Coping with France

'*I think it must have changed hands.*'
Reproduced by courtesy of *Punch*

Coping with France

Fay Sharman

Basil Blackwell

First published 1984
Reprinted 1984
Reprinted with corrections 1985

Basil Blackwell Ltd.
108 Cowley Road, Oxford OX4 1JF, England

Basil Blackwell, Inc.
432 Park Avenue South, Suite 1505,
New York, NY 10016, USA

British Library Cataloguing in Publication Data

Sharman, Fay
  Coping with France.
  1. France – Description and travel – 1975-Guide-books
  1. Title
  914.4'04838   DC16

  ISBN 0-631-13383-6

Library of Congress Cataloging in Publication Data

Sharman, Fay.
  Coping with France.
  Includes index.
  1. France – Description and travel – 1975-Guide-books.
  1. Title
  DC16.S5 1984   914.4'04838   84–16725

  ISBN 0–631-13383-6

Typeset by Cambrian Typesetters, Frimley, Surrey
Printed in Great Britain by Billing and Sons Ltd, Worcester

Contents

Introduction

In appearance, France is much like any other western nation. Its roads and railways, banks, post offices, telephones and supermarkets are recognizable as such. But there is always something indefinably and indisputably French, some element of mystery not yet extinguished by the march of uniformity — the plumbing, for instance. French hotels too are unique. French customs and conventions are a law unto themselves. Even French food, looming so large in the daily routine, can present a challenge to the outsider. And the language, of course, can seem an insuperable hurdle to those who don't know it.

In this book, I have tried to unravel various strands of the French way of life which foreigners such as myself find daunting or strange. It is not a guidebook telling you what to see or where to stay: it is about the practicalities of being in France, and designed to help you deal with everyday situations and encounters. It gives information, advice and, where possible, comfort. I've assumed that the reader is totally unfamiliar with France and may have no knowledge of French and, without tackling the language question in depth, I have aimed to provide a sort of ready reference. Key words and phrases are translated throughout the text, and even if you daren't utter them, you should be able to identify and locate what you need. There are also hints on how to communicate, not necessarily in French.

The book will, I hope, be useful to any English-speaking person going to France, whether bent on pleasure or profit. I have kept in mind the special needs and problems of different types of visitor, wherever they hail from, but it's impossible to cover every category. I have not, for example, said much about long-term residence in France (I resisted the temptation to delve into the legal niceties of French property inheritance). For intending settlers there is plenty of detailed literature available elsewhere.

A few words about the arrangement of the book. It begins with some fairly basic but necessary background on how and when to go to France, which readers will obviously need to supplement with their own detailed research. (The best starting point for this, and for further information on hotels, campsites and so on, is the French Government Tourist Office.) The chapters on driving and travelling around France combine quite routine yet essential facts with helpful hints and recommendations. Food and drink are treated in depth, mainly because they are two of the great and inescapable attractions of France. And the book ends on a more discursive and personal note, offering, I hope, some insight into the French, their characters and their daily life.

Addresses of most organizations mentioned in the book are listed at the end, if you want to follow anything up. There is also a page at the back for suggestions, since there will inevitably be matters I have neglected. Any ideas for improving the book are welcome.

Acknowledgements

I would like to thank the many people who have given advice, encouragement and helpful criticism while the book was being written, and in particular the following: Harriet Barry, Sophie and Claude Bassouls, Philip Carpenter, Brian Chadwick, Michael Davidson, the French Government Tourist Office in London, Robin Hodges, Bénédicte Jayet, M. and Mme. Labonne, Agi Littasy, Barty Phillips, Natasha Rogai, the *syndicat d'initiative* in Ste-Foy-la-Grande.

My thanks also go to the readers who have written in with suggestions, especially P. S. Falla, David Glass, M. R. Green, R. F. Pallett and Thomas F. A. Wiseman.

When to Go – and When Not

The best time to visit France is when its inhabitants are not on holiday — after all, nothing adds greater spice to one's own leisure than the knowledge that everyone else is working, and if you're on business it's more practical. However, this is easier said than done, for the French enjoy the longest holidays in Europe. The legal minimum is now five weeks paid leave per annum, as compared to Britain's three.

French holidays

Les vacances, holidays, are a serious matter for the French, and traditions die hard. The season still starts at the beginning of July and lasts until mid-September, reaching a crescendo between 15 July and the end of August, when something like 80 per cent of the French have their annual month off. A government campaign to stagger the summer break has met with scant success. The French insist on clogging up transport, hotels and campsites in the key months of July and August. The notorious *grand départ*, when every French person gets simultaneously into the car in order to sit in endless traffic jams, occurs on the last Friday of July. It is repeated in reverse (*la rentrée*) at the end of August. In between comes the great change-over of 15 August, which is also a public holiday and the worst possible date to be driving in France. But no one in their right mind, except the French, would travel the roads on any July or August weekend.

The season

The pattern has changed in other respects, not always to the advantage of foreign visitors. Massed Parisians and others decamp, as before, to the south of France, and Brittany continues to be their second favourite goal. But other parts of the country have become almost as crowded in recent years, now that so many more French people can afford a car. Some areas of the Auvergne resemble national fortresses, from which outsiders are barred by hostile hotel-keepers even when there are clearly vacancies. The beaches of the Atlantic coast have gained in popularity too, while the futuristic developments of the Languedoc marshland draw holidaymakers in their thousands.

Paris itself no longer lives up to its morgue-like reputation in August. Most citizens depart, certainly, and many restaurants, shops and theatres shut for the month. But others now stay open to cater for tourists and a summer programme of festivals and events has become well established since 1977, when the office of mayor was restored in the person of Jacques Chirac. August can be one of the pleasantest months to see the sights of the capital, if not to absorb its usually frenetic atmosphere.

Off-season It's essential to book accommodation just about anywhere in France during the high season (see p. 16). Not only is it more crowded then, but it's also more expensive, for many hotels and restaurants cling stubbornly to the habit of opening just for the summer and charging higher rates accordingly. So, it's more sensible to go off peak if you can, but you should check closing times in the Michelin red guide. November can be a particularly bleak month, with even the bakers shutting shop.

School The number of factories that have been persuaded to
holidays and close in July rather than August is very small. However,
weekends the government has managed to spread out school holidays. These take place within the following periods: three weeks in February; three weeks around Easter; five days around Whitsun; the end of June to the first week in September; one week at the end of October and beginning of November; two weeks over Christmas and New Year. The new arrangement enhances the signifiance of the weekend, if it achieves little else.

Within the last decade, Saturday afternoon attendance has been largely abolished in secondary schools, and junior schools now close for the whole weekend. The five-day week is the norm and Saturday has ceased to be a working day in most offices and factories, though not in shops and banks, which tend to shut instead on Mondays (see pp. 23 and 122). The net result has been to heighten the French addiction to *le weekend*, a fairly recent development as the origin of the word shows. City dwellers like to escape to their second home in the country: nearly one in six Frenchmen has access to a second home and France has a higher proportion of them than any other nation. Alternatively, they will drive out to a hotel or to stay with relatives. The effects are most obvious in the regions around Paris. Normandy is close enough to undergo a regular influx of Parisians, with hotels and restaurants booked solid even on winter weekends; in the Yonne department, south of the capital, 20 per cent of all housing consists of second homes.

Travelling and finding accommodation at weekends can be a frustrating business for the foreigner, whatever the time of year. But it is the official holidays or *jours fériés* that cause maximum disruption. France has no less than ten:

Official holidays

New Year's Day (1 January)	Jour de l'An
Easter Sunday and Monday	(Lundi de) Pâques
Labour Day (1 May)	Fête du Travail
Ascension Day (6th Thursday after Easter)	Ascension
Whit Sunday and Monday	(Lundi de) Pentecôte
Bastille Day (14 July)	Quatorze Juillet/Fête Nationale
Assumption Day (15 August)	Assomption/Quinze Août
All Saints Day (1 November)	Toussaint
Armistice Day (11 November)	Armistice
Christmas Day (25 December)	Noël

These are vital dates to bear in mind when planning your trip. First, the banks are shut. Secondly, the traffic is very heavy and particularly so if the holiday falls on a Tuesday or Thursday, in which case many French try to take the Monday or Friday off as well. These holidays have extra sentimental meaning and, on top of the usual weekend pursuits (and congestion), are treated as occasions to be spent with the family. At Toussaint, respects are paid to dear ones already in the grave, even if it involves covering great distances.

On the other hand, the public holidays have less effect on daily life than you might imagine. Most food shops open in the morning, even on Christmas Day; public transport runs; cinemas have performances, though most museums are shut.

Major events in the French calendar

Lists of annual events in France are put out by the French Government Tourist Office each spring. The Michelin green guides also contain a summary of important local happenings. They cover everything from cultural festivals to sporting fixtures, religious ceremonies to folklore fairs. Some are great tourist attractions, others are small in scale. Whether you regard them as an inducement to visit the area or a warning to steer clear is up to you.

Le Mans, for instance, is a notorious bottleneck when motor racing is on and it has many more fixtures than the famous 24 hours in June. It's also worth remembering that France, an ostensibly if not officially Catholic country, abounds in 'holy days'. The feast of its patron saint will bring a town or village to a standstill. And there are numerous dates in the church calendar, like Shrove Tuesday (Mardi Gras), Trinity Sunday (la Fête de la Trinité) and anything connected with the Virgin Mary, that call for local celebrations, even if they are not official holidays.

The weather

The French discuss the weather or *le temps* quite as much as the British are supposed to. But, since so many more depend on agriculture for a livelihood, they have greater justification. Rain and storms, typical of an English August, can ruin the plum harvest in a region like the Dordogne. And France is no exception to the unpredictable behaviour which seems to have overtaken the world's weather. (See p. 154 for weather forcasts.)

Regional variations

It is generally safe to assume that the further south you go the hotter it will be. However, for a country as large as France, the picture is less straightforward. Basically, the Mediterranean region is associated with hot, dry summers and sunny winters, while central and eastern France are subject to continental extremes of heat and cold. The north and west belong, with the British Isles, to the cool temperate zone, which means changeable, rainy, but generally mild; it gets warmer down the Atlantic coast, although still affected by the moisture-laden influence of the ocean.

Local variations and micro-climates complicate the pattern. The Alps protect a corner of the south of France between Nice and the Italian frontier which, before its invasion by the summer masses, was originally a winter haunt of the rich. On this once most exclusive stretch of the Côte d'Azur, Menton still celebrates its fame with the annual lemon festivals of February. In the brilliant winter sunshine of Nice, the thermometer can soar to 35°C (95°F), but will drop sharply at night; this results in an average January temperature on a par with that of Cherbourg in Normandy. Frost and snow are rare on the Riviera coast, whereas inland they are a regular occurrence: you can ski within an hour's drive of the sea. Yet, despite heavy spring showers and autumn storms, the azure clarity of the region is its predominant feature and ample justification for its name.

To the west, Provence as a whole is characterized by dry summer heat and mild winters. It also lies in the path of the *mistral*, a biting northerly wind that whistles down the Rhône valley and strikes Marseille and the Camargue in particular. The island of Corsica, with a very similar climate, suffers from not one but many external winds, among them the *maestrale*, the *sirocco* and the *tramontane*. Its own local breeze, reaching a daily peak around 1 p.m., is known as the *mezzogiorno*. Perversely, the island is hotter in the north than the south.

Along the Mediterranean shore of Languedoc, summers are still reliably very hot and dry, if cooler in the mountains inland. But autumn can arrive suddenly in the form of October frosts and rain; and winters tend to be much colder than in the Riviera, with snow often lying until May. The exception is a belt of land in the shadow of the Pyrenees, roughly from Pau to Carcassonne, blessed with fine, mild conditions from September to December.

In contrast to the arid plateaux of the Roussillon in the east, the Basque country in the west is lush and well watered. From Biarritz to Nantes, the Atlantic coast receives copious rainfall in spring and autumn. Gales can create spectacular rough seas and, although winters are mild, it is colder in the interior. Summers are best here, with hot hazy sunshine tempered by a sea breeze.

Further inland, the Dordogne too owes its verdancy to plentiful rain and is often mild and warm. Eastwards

into the high land of the Massif Central, the weather
becomes less settled, with a number of competing
climates. The mountains make for wetter weather,
notably in April—May and September—October, and for
summer storms. In the northern Massif, the Auvergne is
remarkable for dramatic variations in temperature,
sometimes 20°C (36°F) up or down within a few hours;
the record, a change of 41°C (74°F), occurred at
Clermont-Ferrand on a single August day in 1885. Here,
the continental type of climate is more apparent — severe
winters with snow-blocked roads, sweltering heat in
summer.

The same applies to all eastern France. Burgundy, the
Alps, the Jura, Alsace and Lorraine experience long, hot
summers and lingering, snowy winters, with a lot of rain
at different times. Mountains, again, are an important
factor: the sheltering Vosges can produce suffocating
heat in Alsace.

Northern France is often overhung with that grey,
damp feeling depressingly reminiscent of Britain. Nevertheless, when the sun does shine on the English-looking
Norman orchards, it seems to be imbued with extra
strength and you notice exotic plants like oleanders
growing in cottage gardens. Naturally mild — and wet,
particularly in October — Normandy also enjoys the
warmth of the Gulf Stream, which flows round the
Cotentin peninsula. Brittany is equally moist and mild
throughout the year, though lashed by autumn and
winter gales. On the protected southern shoreline, the
summers are hotter and longer.

Paris in the spring is not just a cliché, and, weather-
wise, April and May are two of the best months there.
Indeed, every region of France has its seasonal charms —
spring flowers in the Jura, apple blossom in Normandy,
the grape harvest in Burgundy, autumn colour in the
Dordogne and Auvergne, snow in the Alps and winter
warmth on the Riviera.

As an overall guide to the best times to visit France,
June and September are probably the safest bets, for
fine weather without the extreme heat (and crowds)
which make people bad-tempered. You won't necessarily
achieve a suntan in the early summer, even in the south,
and the sea can be chilly. By August, the water has really
warmed up, ranging in temperature from 17°C (63°F) in
the Channel, to 19°C (66°F) off the south-west coast, to

23° (73°) on the Côte d'Azur. In October, the Mediterranean is still a bearable 18 or 19° (64°, 66°). But in June
the air is pure, the beaches unsullied, the restaurants
quiet and the evenings long. On the westernmost fringe
of France, in Brittany, the sun never seems to set.

Planning the Trip

This chapter deals with the essential preliminaries for a trip to France. Many of the subjects it touches on are covered in greater detail in subsequent chapters.

Remember to take a dictionary with you. It adds enormously to the interest and pleasure of visiting France. Even if you're reasonably proficient in the language, there are always strange words to look up, particularly when driving (like those mystifying signs everywhere for *brocante*, second-hand furniture or junk). With a dictionary you can also prepare in advance for an encounter in French — instructions to a hotelier perhaps, or a special request to a shopkeeper.

If your French is minimal or non-existent, don't despair. Most everyday activities, such as going to the bank, shopping, eating in a restaurant, can be conducted in blissful ignorance of the language, though of course it helps to have a few French words. You can get by on sign language if necessary, but many more French people know English now and are willing to speak it. Again a dictionary is useful; if you're unable to pronounce the relevant word, you can simply point at it. Phrase books, on the other hand, are not essential. They tend to give long and involved sentences when all you really need is the key word; and they can be positively misleading. (See also the chapter on Communicating.)

Passports and visas

A valid passport is sufficient to admit visitors from most countries to France. It's also the best form of identification when checking into a hotel or campsite or changing money. A visa is rarely required, except for long stays — if in doubt, ask the French consulate.

British visitors' passports

Residents of the UK and Irish Republic may use a British Visitor's Passport. This is obtained quite simply, in contrast to the delaying tactics of the Passport Office, by going to a main post office with the fee, currently £5.50, your birth certificate and medical card or pension book, and two photographs. It lasts for one year and is not renewable.

Daytrippers of British and Irish origin are similarly *Daytripping*
favoured. In theory, you can stay in France for up to 60
hours with an identity card, which is usually arranged
through the cross-Channel operator and issued at the
departure port on production of a photo and a small
payment. However, French customs men can be prone
to irrational nastiness: in a notorious incident in the
summer of 1983, they turned back a boatload of black
visitors with all the correct papers; in another case, they
refused to allow an English couple to carry some German
wine through France in their car, forcing them to catch
the ferry home from Belgium. So you might feel happier
with a proper passport.

If you wish to remain in France longer than three *Resident's*
months, you should apply for a *carte de séjour*, resident's *permits*
permit, from the police several weeks before the three-
month period ends. This must be renewed every three
months.

Vaccinations are not normally necessary, either for **Health and**
entering France or for returning to the US, Canada or **travel**
the UK. But it's sensible to be protected against polio, **insurance**
tetanus, typhoid and cholera when heading for the *Vaccinations*
Mediterranean.

Full medical insurance is strongly recommended. It's *Medical*
particularly important for a winter sports holiday — the *expenses*
last thing you want to think about as you lie in the snow
with a broken leg is the huge cost of being rescued by
the blood wagon.

Treatment in France is subsidized by the state. the
French citizen pays the medical bill in full and is then
reimbursed most of it (see p. 30 for further details). But
for the average visitor, who can't benefit from this
system, doctors' and dentists' charges, hospital bills,
ambulance trips and medicines are all expensive. A visit
to the doctor's surgery or office currently costs 65f
and one to a specialist 95f. It is in fact a criminal offence
in France not to go to the aid of someone in distress,
so you wouldn't be left in the street to die because
you were penniless. However, it's not advisable to rely
on this small crumb of comfort.

North Americans are often covered worldwide for
medical expenses, but should check their policies. Most
Britons will have to invest in special health insurance,
which can usually be combined with travel cover (against

cancellation, loss of possessions, inconvenience through accident or injury and so on). Tour operators, motoring organizations and insurance companies offer various schemes.

UK residents can also take advantage of the reciprocal agreement for health care between Britain and France. Under this scheme, a magical form known as E111 puts you on the same footing as a French citizen within the French national health service. It entitles you to recover about 80 per cent of the cost of medical bills and prescription charges incurred in France, however much these amount to. (Similar provisions exist for all EEC countries.)

Details of the agreement are set out in a Department of Health and Social Security leaflet, together with an application for form E111. Technically, you must be in employment or a pensioner to qualify, although there are loopholes which the unemployed and self-employed can pursue with the DHSS — and a measure of patience.

It does involve tangling with French, as well as British, bureaucracy, if you claim a refund using your form E111 (see p. 32 for the somewhat lengthy procedure). And when you read the DHSS regulations telling you to take the form to French social security *before* the doctor, you may wonder whether it's worth the bother. Unless you are intending a long stay in France, it probably isn't and most people will find a private health insurance policy perfectly adequate.

For additional documents needed by motorists, see p. 42.

Currency   Money is, I'm afraid, essential, in one form or another (see p. 21). It's a good idea to carry some loose change, as well as cheque book and credit cards. Better, too, to purchase your francs from a bank at home, rather than queuing on the boat or at the airport, inevitably for a lower rate of exchange and higher commission.

There is no limit to the amount you can bring in to France. But, if you're likely to leave with banknotes to the value of 5,000f or more, you should state your intention to the customs authorities on arrival, and fill in the relevant form.

Getting there   Looking across the Straits of Dover on a clear day, it's
by sea   possible to distinguish the Continent on the other side, a black line low on the horizon. Less than 25 miles

separate Britain from France and yet these miles have the significance of an unbridgeable gulf, historically, culturally, and even technically, as the Channel tunnel project has never advanced further than paper.

The Channel is the most expensive stretch of water in the world in terms of transport costs, and, starting from the UK, you can't avoid it. However, competition between the cross-Channel operators ensures plenty of special deals, discounts and promotional fares, which are well worth researching before you decide on a route.

Ferries

The main companies are Sealink and Seaspeed, the cross-Channel sector of British Rail; Townsend Thoresen; P & O Ferries; Sally Line; and Brittany Ferries, founded in 1973 by a cooperative of Breton farmers to export their vegetables and import tourists. In the old days, one hoped for a French-run boat, with authentic coffee and croissants, a five-course lunch, Armagnac and Calvados in the bar: France began as soon as the ferry cast off from the English shore. But today the ferries are uniformly functional, built to hold a thousand passengers or more and their cars, and equipped with cafeterias and restaurants, bars and lounges, discos and cinemas, duty-free and souvenir boutiques, fruit machines, video games and drink dispensers. Muzak competes with hoardes of schoolchildren on educational trips to prevent anyone sleeping who has not bought a reclining seat or cabin.

Hovercraft

The alternative is the hovercraft, which can 'fly' the Channel in half an hour. It is presented to customers as an aircraft instead of a seagoing vessel, no doubt to conceal its sick-making qualities. Not for the claustrophobic, either, but it's certainly fast.

Hydrofoil

Sadly, there is only one hydrofoil service now, between the Channel Islands and St Malo. Smooth, quiet and quick, it's one of the nicest modes of travel, although more affected by weather conditions.

French ports

If much of the romance has been removed from crossing the Channel, the ports have not lost their charm, especially Dieppe and St Malo. There are four major routes to France — Dover or Folkestone to Calais or Boulogne, shortest and cheapest and most frequent; Ramsgate to Dunkerque, two and a half hours; Newhaven to Dieppe, just under four; and the longer hauls — up to nine hours from Southampton, Portsmouth, Weymouth or Plymouth to Cherbourg, Le Havre, St Malo or Roscoff.

For the motorist, the choice of crossing depends on the point of departure in Britain and the ultimate destination. The fastest sea route is not, in fact, the most economical and even less so when it entails a long drive through France, with petrol, meals and accommodation to add to the basic fare. Road connections are another factor. Boulogne, Calais, Dunkerque and Le Havre are accessible by motorway, whereas the rest are not. On the other hand, the motorway could mean having to negotiate a route round Paris.

For the unmotorized traveller, it's more a question of personal inclination. Most of the French ports contain good shops, markets and hypermarkets, hotels and restaurants. Calais and Boulogne have efficient road and rail links with the capital, but lack the atmosphere which makes other towns more desirable for a long weekend.

Cheap fares There are lots of money-saving dodges for getting across the Channel. To benefit from lower tariffs, travel out of the high season, July and August, and mid-week rather than weekends, holiday weekends in particular. You miss the crowds as well and are less likely to fall victim to striking seamen. Caravans go at a much reduced rate outside peak periods. Fares are cheaper too if you don't mind disembarking at an unsociable time, like three in the morning on the short routes or early evening after an all-day voyage.

Excusion tickets, for 48, 60 or 120 hours in France, are much less than the normal fare and the ferry companies are quite flexible, within an hour or two, about the deadline for the return sailing. One obvious way to spread costs is to pack a car with as many consenting adults as possible. Large groups can also claim discounts. Prices for the vehicle itself are usually calculated on its length, but not always, so it pays to shop around if you have a big car. Bicycles are very cheap to transport, sometimes free, and the same applies to motorbikes.

From further afield The Channel is not the only waterway to France and you can get there from further afield by ocean-going liner, freighter with passenger accommodation or cruise ship. From North America the most regular crossings are

by Cunard to Le Havre and Cherbourg, often via Southampton where foot passengers may embark for a Channel
trip in style. Merchant lines ply between ports in the
USA and Canada and Europe, and from South Africa to
Marseille.

Scheduled airlines fly to Paris from all over the world.   **Getting there**
There are frequent services from major cities in the US,   **by air**
Montreal and Toronto, Sydney, Johannesburg, and from
European capitals. A few stop over in Nice.

From the UK, Air France and British Airways fly
direct to several cities as well as Paris. Although France
restricts the number of charter companies, there are
some, and many flights start from provincial airports in
addition to Heathrow and Gatwick.

On the scheduled airlines, promotional fares like Apex
generally require advance booking. From Britain, you
should be able to pick up a cheaper scheduled flight
through a tour operator or travel agent, but savings are
not great.

If you fly from New York to Nice on an ordinary
ticket, you may stop off at various European cities
without extra charge.

For details of the domestic French air system, which
is very good, see p. 65.

As a method of journeying to and around France, the   **Getting there**
train has much to commend it. It's one of the finest   **by rail**
ways of observing any country, absorbing the local
flavour and mingling with the natives; it brings a sense of
adventure and achievement, so that you feel like a real
traveller instead of a tripper; and, with concessions
available for just about everyone, it need not be expensive.

Rail links are reasonable on both sides of the Channel
(for details in France, see p. 61). It's quite easy to travel
from any station in Britain, boarding a train to one of
the ports, catching a ferry or hovercraft, and then
hopping on the first train to Paris or wherever. For the
foot passenger, the fastest route is via Dover—Boulogne,
with a direct rail link to Paris.

Alternatively, you can buy a through ticket combining
train and Channel crossing. Paris is the best served
destination, and the London to Paris boat train takes as
little as eight hours. Trains with sleeping accommodation
also run from Calais to the south of France all year;

reservations for a bed or bunk are compulsory when you buy the ticket, though you might find last-minute cancellations on the spot.

Paris and the main cities are well served by trains from the rest of Europe, as part of the Eurail network. Among them are the super-duper Trans Europ Express (TEE) trains, for air-conditioned, sound-proofed luxury at a supplement. Eurail timetables are on sale at most continental stations; train buffs will doubtless be armed with Thomas Cook's famous international timetable.

Motorail   Motorists from the UK might consider using Motorail, if they can afford it. Car or motorbike and people are transported by rail through France, the latter in sleepers or couchettes for an additional payment, but with meals included. The service operates from Calais, Boulogne, Dieppe and Paris to the west, centre, south and east. Return journeys must be booked, although you can come back from a different Motorail terminal.

Cheap fares   Rail bargains abound, and not only for students and pensioners. Anyone who is neither French nor resident in France can take advantage of France Vacances. This rover ticket from SNCF (French railways) entitles the holder to unlimited rail travel in France, first or second class, for 7 or 15 days or a month. The cheapest version cost £70 in 1984. As it is exclusively for foreign holiday-makers, it must be bought before you enter France. Further perks of France Vacances are a reduction on SNCF coach excursions; unrestricted use of public transport in Paris; entrance to the Paris Beaubourg centre; and, in the case of first-class rovers, free car rental for one or two days from certain stations.

European residents under 26 can purchase a Carte Interail. This gives a month's free rail travel anywhere in Europe except the home country, where half price is paid. The half fare extends to Sealink ferries for UK nationals.

Senior citizens of any nationality can claim a 30 per cent reduction on all continental rail fares with a Carte Vermeil. For those from the UK, a full Railcard allows half-price travel in the British Isles and 30 per cent off Sealink and European trains.

The Eurailpass is for North American residents. This is a first-class rover ticket providing unlimited rail travel in 13 European countries for various periods, plus discounts on other services. The Eurail Youthpass is a similar deal, second class, for those under 26. Both may be purchased in the States or Canada, or at the SNCF offices in London and Paris.

Transalpino in London do rail tickets at special rates for young people. Members of the Youth Hostels Association should inquire about lower fares from the YHA. Savings can also be made on tickets bought within France (see p. 63).

Getting there by road

Coaching

Coaches have become a very cheap form of transport, with fares sometimes less than a quarter those of the train. With the expansion of services in Britain, there are now reliable connections to ports and airports for crossing the Channel. However, coaching is an uncertain choice for independent travel on the other side, as France does not have a comparable system of long-distance buses.

If you do go by coach from the UK, it's safer to buy a through ticket. These can be obtained for a wide variety of routes, not only between the two capitals, but from different parts of the UK to places in France which may be difficult to reach by other means. Regular services from London are operated by Euroways and Riviera Express.

Europabus, run by a consortium of the European railways, is one of the chief operators in continental coach travel. They have a luxury fleet with English-speaking guides. You can either take an inclusive tour, or catch one of their coaches, break your journey and continue on a different one. Meals and overnight accommodation may be booked in advance.

Coach tours of the continent, inclusive of air fare, can be booked from the US. But it's probably easier and cheaper to organize from Britain.

Driving

For drivers from elsewhere in Europe, road communications are excellent. Motorways lead into France from all neighbouring countries. (See the chapter on Driving.)

Packages

The great advantage of France, for the British anyway, is the fact that you can simply jump in the car, get on the ferry, drive to a pleasant spot and put up at the nearest welcoming hostelry, all more or less on impulse.

Nevertheless, the tour operators vie with each other to look after you. There is a vast selection of packages, designed for every imaginable taste and covering every region of France from Flanders to Corsica, in all possible permutations of transport. Anything goes — conventional resort holidays with travel, transfer and hotel; self-catering, caravanning, camping, boating, transport thrown in and on-site equipment if you want; motoring jaunts, with chosen hotels or 'go-as-you-please'; inclusive trips to Paris; coach tours; shopping excursions; and special interest, from art and archaeology to war graves, windsurfing and wine.

The French Government Tourist Office in London publishes a comprehensive listing of tour operators, together with a price guide. Among these is the French Travel Service, the package arm of SNCF. Its programme, based on rail or air travel, includes the second-class return train fare from any British Rail station to London. FTS also offers a discount on car rental.

For visitors to France from other parts of the world, a travel agent is indispensable, if only to reserve tranport and accommodation. This assistance should be free; naturally, you pay for a tailor-made itinerary with all the trimmings.

From North America, there is an assortment of packages, often of the grander Champagne-and-Rolls-Royce kind. It may be cheaper to book a special interest holiday from Britain. Again, the starting point for information is the French Government Tourist Office in your country.

Booking accommodation
Even if you're travelling fancy-free, you might want to fix up accommodation in advance, whether for an overnight stop or a base for the week. In the high season, reservations are essential, especially for popular places, and should be made well ahead. Booking is advisable for Paris at any time of year: in 1983, the capital was reportedly saturated by June.

A hotel or campsite will be the choice of most people (see pp. 78 and 88). But there are many alternative types of accommodation — holiday villages, youth hostels, lodging with a family, monasteries and convents (nearly a hundred accept paying guests). The French Government Tourist Office can put you on the right track or in touch with the relevant organization. The Club Méditerranée, for instance, has offices in the UK and US. The FGTO cannot undertake actual reservations.

However, Loisirs-Accueil is a special booking service which reserves accommodation of all kinds, as well as inclusive and special interest holidays. It has about 30 branches in France open thoughout the year, most of them with English-speaking staff. The FGTO will supply addresses.

Firms specializing in on-site tents, caravans and mobile homes are also listed by the French Government Tourist Office. They usually throw in the Channel crossing. From the USA, you can rent camper vans for collection in Europe.

For self-catering, see p. 84.

Going through customs

Arriving in France by whatever means, you will have to go through customs, *douane*. You will be asked to present your *passeport*, and other documents if in a car, and whether you have anything to declare — *Avez-vous quelque chose à déclarer? Rien* is the answer if you have nothing.

The customs officials will probably address you in French but will almost certainly know some English, which they can resort to if necessary. They might inquire about the purpose of your visit, where you have come from and are going, and how long you are staying. You may also be asked to complete a form, repeating the information in your passport.

Allowances on entering France

All visitors are allowed to bring in personal effects like clothing and jewellery without paying duty or tax. Anything obviously intended for your own use is also exempt, including two cameras and ten films and a musical instrument. (For regulations on cars, see p. 42.)

A Citizen's Band radio may be imported temporarily into France, but the set should be of a type approved in the UK. British owners of such equipment must hold a British Telecom licence showing the agreement number.

If you want to take a metal detector in, it's wise to obtain a form known as *un acquit à caution* to facilitate procedure through customs. So long as it is purely a hobby, no permit is required.

Animals are admitted to France, provided they have certificates of health and anti-rabies vaccinations. Nevertheless, it is much safer, and kinder, not to transport pets. Rabies is endemic in Europe and the rules are strict, especially for Britain which has so far escaped the disease. It is an offence to bring an animal or bird into the UK without an import licence, which is issued in advance and requires 6 months' quarantine of the creature. Penalties are severe for both humans and animals.

Returning home
It is the duty-free allowance on things like cigarettes and drink that concerns most people. Leaflets distributed to travellers and posters in the customs halls explain the regulations; it helps to find out about them on the way out, so that you can plan your purchases for the return.

For the British, the crucial distinction to bear in mind hinges on the source of these articles. They fall into two categories:

1 goods bought in the ordinary way in a shop within the EEC, duty and tax paid (i.e. hidden in the price) — the higher allowance;
2 goods bought free of duty and tax within the EEC, in other words in a duty-free shop on the boat or place or at the airport; and goods bought outside the EEC — the lower allowance.

Member states of the EEC, besides France and Britain, are Belgium, Denmark, West Germany, Greece, Irish Republic, Italy, Luxembourg and the Netherlands. The Channel Islands do not belong to the Community.

Goods are divided into groups, namely tobacco products, alcoholic drinks, perfume, toilet-water, and other goods. The point is that you cannot mix allowances for the two categories within the same group of articles. For example, if you buy a litre of duty-free whisky on the boat, you are automatically restricted to the lower allowance of category 2 for the whole of your drinks quota; this means only an additional 2 litres of still table wine instead of the 4 you would have been entitled to under category 1. On the other hand, there's nothing to prevent you buying your cigarettes duty-free and your alcohol in a shop in France, since these belong to separate groups.

A word about the definition of drinks. Spirits — whisky, gin, vodka, rum, brandy, Pernod, Calvados — and most liqueurs are normally over 22% volume or 38.8° proof. *Cassis, fraise,* advocaat and many aperitifs may be less. Among the fortified wines are sherry, port, madeira and vermouth. Sparkling wines include Champagne and the like, and also the semi-sparkling, identified in French by the words *mousseux*, *crémant*, *pétillant*, *perlant* and *perlé*. The label should give details of alcoholic strength and the size of the bottle.

The cross-Channel ferry companies encourage you to purchase your duty-frees on board; on longer routes, they prolong the voyage so that the boutiques can open at some unearthly hour before docking. But, in the drinks department, the range is unimaginative and not necessarily cheap. Many people prefer to resist these blandishments and devote the entire alcohol allowance to wine bought in France. This entitles you to 7 litres, or 9 bottles of 73 cl capacity, the most common French size, with a quarter litre over. Customs officials usually ignore a bottle on the go. If you exceed the limit, you will have to pay about £1 in duty per bottle, but this can be worthwhile when buying in bulk (see p. 120).

Under the 'other goods' umbrella you may bring into the UK 2 kg fruit or vegetables (not potatoes because of Colorado beetle); 5 plants (not chrysanthemums, bulbs or fruit trees); 1 small bunch of cut flowers; 50 litres of beer; 1 kg fresh meat (not pork, offal or poultry); 1 kg ham or dried sausage or cooked meat. However, the British authorities want to discourage people from bringing back uncooked meat and meat products; these must be declared to customs.

Other countries have different laws for homecoming travellers. The US has its own quirks, which citizens should be familiar with; you can bring in one US quart of alcohol, for instance, but only if your gateway state permits it and you are over 21. At the opposite extreme, Canadian babies may import their quota of tobacco.

Avoiding VAT

Visitors can claim exemption from French value-added tax (*TVA* in French) on items costing more than a certain amount which they have bought in France. At present, this applies to single purchases over 1,030f if you are resident in the EEC, and to purchases totalling more than 800f if you live elsewhere. Shops are not legally obliged to offer this service, although many do in Paris and larger towns. The assistant will fill in a sales docket and hand you duplicates. These must be presented to customs when you leave France, which is a time-consuming business, and the officials will probably want to inspect the article as well. Eventually, you should receive a refund in the post.

If you're from overseas and not a Common Market resident, you can avoid paying value-added tax on most of your shopping. Ask the shop to send your goods direct to your home address, or alternatively to your point of departure from France where you can collect them.

Money, Post and Telephones

The widespread acceptance of credit cards, together with the introduction of Eurocheques and Eurocheque cards, have made travellers' cheques almost redundant. However, money in all these forms, as well as straight cash, can be changed at most banks in France. Many hotels have exchange facilities, but their rates are likely to be less favourable, especially in the holiday season and at weekends. In Paris, *bureaux de change* at the airports are open 24 hours a day.

Money

A lot of people, particularly Americans, still feel safer with travellers' cheques (same word in French, or sometimes *chèques de voyage*). Overall, it is cheaper to have the individual cheques in large amounts, as you normally have to pay a small fee each time you cash one. They can be denominated in either your own currency or an internationally accepted one, such as dollars or sterling, and are cashed at the current exchange rate; or in French francs, in which case the rate is fixed at the time of purchase. The choice depends on the number of countries you plan to visit and on your expectation of the way exchange rates will move. Travellers' cheques are available from banks — not necessarily your own bank — and from post offices, building societies and firms like American Express and Thomas Cook.

Travellers' cheques

Travellers' cheques do have the merit of being difficult to cash if stolen, and often they can be quickly refunded if lost. They have a sort of ring of reliability, which might make them easier to change in remote places or outside banking hours, even more so if they are in francs. The reason is, of course, that you have already bought them and they represent actual currency, at a price. The hole in your account is there in advance. In France, however, they are not accepted on the same scale as in the USA.

Credit cards are sweeping Europe somewhat later than America, but the French no longer look askance at them, except in a few areas off the tourist track. They

Credit cards

may be tendered in restaurants, hotels, service stations, garages, shops, supermarkets, wherever you see the relevant sign. Check in the Michelin red guide to find out which credit cards are accepted by a particular hotel or restaurant. They may also be drawn on as a source of cash, although some banks are less cooperative about this.

The most common cards are Carte Bleue (Visa, Barclaycard); Eurocard (MasterCard, Access); Diner's Club; and American Express. 'La Carte Bleue' sometimes means credit cards in general.

The great plus point of credit cards abroad is the time-lag. Your account is debited not on the day of the transaction but when it filters through to your home country, perhaps weeks later, giving you plenty of time before you have to pay. Similarly, the rate of exchange to be charged is usually determined on the debit date at your bank and, in the case of cash advances, the interest is calculated only from then.

Make sure you know what to do if your card is lost while abroad. Often the first step is to notify the nearest bank with the appropriate sign for your particular credit card.

Eurocheque cards and Eurocheques

Eurocheque cards (sometimes known as 'Eurocards' but not the same as the credit card) and Eurocheques have superseded the old system whereby British travellers could obtain money abroad with banker's card and cheque book. They are designed to give greater security against fraud.

The banks have opted for two arrangements — either a Eurocheque encashment card which guarantees ordinary cheques; or a Eurocheque card to be used in conjunction with special Eurocheques. The advantage of the latter is that they can be handed over in payment at hotels, shops, garages etc., as well as providing a means of getting cash.

The cheque should be written out in £s, or the Euro-cheque in francs, and presented with cheque book and card at any bank displaying the Eurocheque symbol. You are allowed to draw two cheques up to £50 in any one day. Card-holders will probably be able to use cash dispensers in the near future as well.

You must order the card and/or cheques from your bank in advance. Commission is charged on each transaction in the normal way. Unlike travellers' cheques, however, the Eurocheque card enables you to pace your spending. It also works out cheaper. If you lose the card, inform your bank branch at home immediately.

The National Girobank in Britain has also introduced a foreign cheque card, which can be used at post offices abroad.

Don't forget to arm yourself with enough francs for initial expenses when you arrive in France. Bear in mind bank closing times (see below) when working out how much cash to take. *Cash*

French banknotes come in the following denominations — 500, 200, 100, 50, 20 and 10 francs. They depict great Frenchmen in a colourful way (the artist Delacroix, for instance, clearly modelled on Dirk Bogarde).

There are 100 centimes to one franc. Centime coins are brassy and come in units of 5, 10 and 20. Francs are silvery, in units of ½, 1, 2 and 5, and coppery for the 10f piece. This is slightly larger than the 1f coin, but thicker and heavier, and has virtually supplanted the 10f note.

You will find that you end up with pockets full of change in France. Don't get flustered counting it out in a shop: the French take ages themselves, but they are appreciative if you give the correct amount.

Banking hours in France are generally 9 a.m. to 12 noon or 12.30, and 2 p.m. to 4 or 5 p.m. In Paris and big towns, banks sometimes stay open through lunch and in the evening until 7. **Banks**

Opening times

All banks are closed on Sundays and public holidays. Very often, they shut at midday the day before a public holiday and for the whole of the following day — most infuriating if you have never heard of Assumption Day, for instance. Many banks also catch you out by closing on a Monday, although others more predictably choose Saturday to shut. In Paris, most banks close on Saturdays, apart from a few foreign ones and exchange bureaux. Banks tend to stay open when there's a Saturday market in a town, for all those rich farmers to stash away their loot. Branches of Crédit Agricole often operate on Saturdays.

Recognizing   *Banques* are remarkable for their glamour. The chrome
a French bank   and tinted glass can look incongruous in the setting of a
provincial backwater, where the majority of customers
are local peasants with mud on their boots. But the
modern architecture is a sign of the great expansion in
French banking since the 1960s, with the creation of
new branches both in France and abroad. Four of the
world's top ten banks are French — the Banque Nationale
de Paris, Crédit Lyonnais and Société Générale, all state
controlled, and, largest of all, the Crédit Agricole. Yet it
is only recently that cheque books have become
common among the French. It is an offence to overdraw
an account in France, which is why cheques are always
acceptable.

Trying to enter a French bank can be disconcerting.
Many of them, particularly in smart resorts, keep the
front door locked. You have to ring the bell and wait to
be sized up before a buzzer is pressed and you are
admitted.

Inside, you go to one counter for the transaction and
are directed to another, *la caisse*, cashier's desk, to
collect the money. Large banks sometimes have a separate
change or *bureau de change* section.

You can ask to *encaisser un chèque*, cash a cheque, or
changer de l'argent, change some money. *La monnaie*,
however, is small change. Take your passport for identification.

Prices   Prices are usually written $2,50^F$ — 2 francs 50 centimes;
or $0,50^F$ — half a franc, or 50 centimes.

Old francs, or *anciens francs* were abolished years
ago, when it was decreed that 100 old francs should
equal 1 new franc, and that 1 old franc should equal 1
new centime. Nevertheless, sometimes the French quote
prices in *anciens francs*, which can be upsetting. For
example, $1,40^F$ might be written as 140^F and you
would be asked for *cent quarante* instead of *un franc
quarante*. If you're suspicious, simply remove the last
couple of noughts or move the decimal comma back two
places to translate into *nouveaux francs*. House prices
are often given in millions of old francs.

Watch out for the southern accent, which can make
cent (100) sound like *cinq* (5).

Paying bills   In restaurants, cafés and bars, you should request *l'addition, s'il vous plaît*, the bill, please, but in most other places, like hotels and garages, the bill is *la note*. A receipt is *un reçu*. (See also pp. 83 and 106.)

Service is almost invariably included in restaurant and hotel bills, except in Paris where they have a nasty habit of quoting prices minus the extras. This is indicated on the menu, tariff, list of charges or bill itself by *STC*, sometimes spelt out *service et taxe compris* (service and tax included), *SC* or *service compris, tout compris* (all included), or *prix nets* (net prices).

Service charges, tipping and tax

In bars and cafés, it's less straightforward. These must by law display a price list, which should tell you whether service is included; failing that, the bill should say. As a rule, service is included if you sit down at a table, but is excluded if you stand at the bar. In that case, leave a 12½ per cent tip in the plastic dish on the counter.

Otherwise, tipping is really a matter for your own discretion and much the same as in other countries. Taxi drivers, porters, chambermaids, cloakroom attendants, hairdressers, barbers, tour and museum guides all expect *un pourboire*, a tip. If you move in the world of wine waiters and hotel commissionaires, you will know that they do too. Service station assistants who clean your windscreen are not waiting for a gratuity, but will be pleased if one is offered.

The only unexpected categories are usherettes in cinemas and theatres and at sporting events like tennis matches.

TVA stands for *taxe sur la valeur ajoutée* and means, in the usual inverted French style, VAT or value added tax. It is levied on most goods and services, normally at a rate of 18.6 per cent.

Unlike the USA and, more recently, Britain, the postal and telephone systems in France are run by the same government department, the Ministère des Postes, Téléphones et Télécommunications. Yellow is the identifying colour for the little Renault or Citroën mail vans and post boxes, although the *facteur* or postman wears a grey outfit too casual to qualify as uniform. The logo looks like a handmade paper dart against a fluttering teatowel, enclosed in a circle.

The postal system

The post office In large towns, the typical post office is an imposing edifice which could be mistaken for the town hall or police station. Inside are the lines of patient people, sulky staff and 'position closed' notices that seem to be a feature of post offices worldwide. With luck, there might be separate *guichets*, 'counters', for stamps and more lengthy transactions.

It is possible and infinitely preferable to avoid the post office altogether. But, if you must visit it, you should ask or look out for the *PTT* ('pay-tay-tay'), *PT* or *P et T, bureau de poste* or *postes*. Your reason might be to send a parcel (*un colis*), register a letter (*recommander une lettre*), obtain a postal order (*un mandat-poste*) or international money order (*un mandat international*), or consult a telephone directory (*un annuaire*).

Other business, namely buying stamps, posting a letter, sending a telegram and making a phone call, can be conducted without recourse to the post office. You can, of course, use it for these purposes and, for more detailed information such as postal rates to Timbuctoo, you will have to.

Poste restante facilities are available at main post offices. Tell your correspondents to write to you *Poste restante* at the Poste Centrale, followed by the postal code of the *département* and the name of the town, and remind them not to put 'Esq.' after the name, which could get you pigeonholed under E. You need to show your passport and pay a small fee when collecting the mail (*le courrier*). You can leave a forwarding address before you move on. American Express and Thomas Cook will also hold letters for people travelling with them.

Opening times Post office opening hours are 8 a.m. to 7 p.m. Monday to Friday, and 8 to 12 noon on Saturday. Most close between 12 or 12.30 and 2. In Paris there is one post office open per *arrondissement* (or borough) on Sunday, from 8 to 11 a.m. The central post office in the capital, at 52 rue du Louvre, never closes.

Posting a letter *Le tabac*, tobacconist's, instantly recognizable by a sort of red carrot outside, sells *timbres*, stamps. It often stocks *cartes postales*, postcards, as well. Stamps can be bought at the post office, of course, and from yellow vending machines outside some post offices.

To the UK, air mail is automatic so a *par avion* sticker is not required. Surface mail is *ordinaire*.

Post boxes are found inside and outside the post office, near tobacconists and elsewhere. They are yellow, either on a pillar or set discreetly into a wall. Post boxes can be difficult to locate: ask for *la boîte postale*.

For urgent letters, go to the station post box. In Paris, you can send letters by the *pneumatique*, using a separate box so labelled, which guarantees delivery within the capital in three hours. In country areas, there is one collection a day and one delivery.

Otherwise, the French postal service is fairly inefficient. It might take anything up to ten days from France to Britain or the States. Within France, the situation is no better: you can't rely on first-class letters being delivered the next day, and second-class can take weeks to reach their destination.

During the last ten years or so, smart perspex kiosks have sprouted throughout France, in streets and squares and often attached to bus stops. The public phone box has finally arrived. At the same time, there has been a dramatic improvement in the French telephone system as a whole. The network is now almost completely automated and internationally linked, and it's feasible to call Los Angeles, Melbourne or Manchester from the depths of the French countryside.

Telephones

Public phones

You can still, of course, go to the post office to make a call; or you can use a café or hotel telephone, for which there's a surcharge to the official rate. But the great attraction of the new public phones, especially for non-French-speakers, is that they are automatic and therefore impersonal.

These phone boxes accept 1f, 5f and 50c coins. Instructions are displayed in English and other languages as well as French. Basically, you lift the receiver, put in the money, wait for the dialling tone and dial. More coins can be fed in during the call and a flashing light warns when the money is running out. Any surplus money will be returned at the end of the call. If it doesn't work you are entitled to claim a refund from the nearest post office, assuming you can prove your honesty and identity. You can only dial by putting the money in first. So you have to pay, even for an emergency call or to get the operator. But then it is an offence in France not to have money on you (see p. 35).

Direct
dialling

On the whole, and unlike its postal counterpart, the telephone service is effective. You normally get through first time. However, you have to get accustomed to the peculiar sounds emitted by French phones — a high-pitched dialling tone, long bleeps for ringing, and rapid shorter ones for 'engaged' (*tonalité*). It is essential to dial quickly without pausing between numbers.

For international calls, dial 19, wait for the continuous buzzing tone, then dial the national code (1 for the USA and Canada, 44 for the UK, 61 for Australia, 27 for South Africa), followed by the area code (but omitting the first 0 for Britain, e.g. 1 not 01 for London) and the subscriber's number.

All areas in France have a departmental code. To make a call to another *département*, first dial 16, wait for the tone change, then dial the two-digit departmental code, followed by the six-digit number. To call Paris from the provinces, start with 16 again, then dial 1 and the seven-digit number.

Local calls are those within a *département*, where you simply dial the six-digit number, or seven-digit within Paris.

Cheap rate

Cheap rate in France and for all Common Market countries is 9 p.m. to 8 a.m., and all day on Sundays and public holidays. For the USA and Canada, it is 10 p.m. to 10 a.m., as well as Sundays and holidays.

For police and ambulance, dial 17; fire 18. You have to put money in, as already explained.

Operator
service

For the operator, dial 13.

Use the same number to make a reversed charge or collect call. This is known as *PCV* ('pay-say-vay', for *percevoir*). Person-to-person (i.e. when you specify a particular person you want to talk to and are charged only if you are connected to that person), *avec préavis* or *PAV*, is also 10. These calls are charged at a higher rate than usual.

For directory inquiries, dial 12.

To send a telegram (*un télégramme*), dial 14. The minimum charge is for 10 words in France, 7 words abroad. You can also send a telegram from a post office.

Telephone
talk

Le numéro, the number, is quoted as it is written: 12—34—56 is *douze, trente-quatre, cinquante-six* —

twelve, thirty-four, fifty-six (not one, two, three . . . as an English person would say). 0 is *zéro*.

The polite French greeting on the phone is *allô*, uttered with a question mark. To check that you have the right number, say *le 12—34—56?*

The operator will use phrases like *ne quittez pas* or *ne bougez pas*, hold on; *j'essaie de vous passer l'abonné*, trying to connect you; and *parlez*, go ahead, talk.

From abroad, you can call any six-digit number in France, or seven-digit in the Paris region, on international direct dialling. Dial the code for France, then the *département* code and subscriber's number.   *Phoning France*

Emergencies and Advice

The fact of being in a foreign country magnifies mishaps into disasters, and it's not just the unfamiliarity of the surroundings. A stolen handbag or wallet, for instance, will probably contain most of your worldly wealth, passport and travel tickets; and the sort of cold you would put up with at home can ruin a precious fortnight's holiday.

As already mentioned, it's madness to travel without adequate insurance. Cover for accident, injury or illness is essential and, if you're driving, so is vehicle protection. A policy for loss or theft of possessions is advisable as well.

This chapter deals with various contingencies, from being arrested to losing your way, and also explains some sources of help and advice on all kinds of matters. (For emergencies on the road and in the home, see pp. 50 and 88.)

Health — or, rather, ill-health

France devotes more of the national budget to health than to either education or defence, and the number of doctors has roughly doubled in the last twenty years. So you might think it was a good place in which to fall ill. You would be deceived.

In the first place, much of the expenditure on health is eaten up by medicines, which the French even more than Americans, are especially partial to. Under the French system, the patient pays the prescription charge at the pharmacy and then claims the money back from social security. The usual refund is 70 per cent but, for the more expensive drugs which many doctors prescribe, the state often gives total reimbursement. The cost of keeping the French in drugs leaves little in the health kitty for hospitals. France spends less in this sphere than any comparable country.

In the second place, the expansion of the medical profession means that doctors have to compete with each other for custom, in order to earn a living. There is a set fee for a consultation (65f in 1984), three-quarters of which is recovered by the patient from the government. The most popular doctor with the French is the one who is generous with prescriptions, or else refers them to a good specialist. These, too, have multiplied, specializing in rheumatology, cardiac disease, cancer and other modern complaints. They can charge double, or more, the rate of an ordinary doctor.

On top of all this, pharmacists have a monopoly of the sale of medicines and can impose a hefty mark-up. Prices may be as much as four times the wholesale value and will certainly seem high to Britons.

Americans will already be conversant with the arguments against pay-as-you-suffer medicine. But if you've been brought up on the National Health and have the misfortune to need treatment in France, you could be in for more of a shock.

However, there are advantages. As a patient, you can shop around for a doctor and seek a second or third opinion. You can also go straight to a specialist, without an intermediary. French doctors, unlike American ones, welcome being called out to visit you, as they get paid extra. And, because there are more of them, there's less queuing at the surgery or office. Moreover, hospitals have improved dramatically in recent years: most of them are now in modern buildings, well equipped and staffed, and waiting lists are minimal.

Calling an ambulance

For *une ambulance*, dial 17. You probably won't have to pay. Emergency numbers are listed in the front of the phone book, and include the Centre Anti-Poisons, for treatment for poisoning.

Consulting a doctor

If you need to find a doctor, look up *médecins* in the yellow pages of the phone directory or inquire at the pharmacy, social security office, police station or tourist office. H is the sign for *un hôpital*, often known as *CHU* (*centre hospitalier universitaire*) or *CHR* (*centre hospitalier régional*). The casualty or emergency department is *les urgences*.

Male or female, a doctor is always *un médecin*. He or she is addressed as *docteur*, or *le docteur X* or, more formally, *Monsieur* or *Madame le docteur X*. (*Médecin*) *généraliste* on the brass plate outside means a general practitioner, and *le cabinet* (*de consultation*) is the surgery or consulting room. A surgeon is *un chirurgien*.

Having reached the doctor, it might seem superfluous to state that you're ill — *Je suis malade*. However, there's a simple phrase to indicate the cause of the trouble — *J'ai mal*, followed by the painful area, *à l'estomac, à la gorge, au pied, aux dents* (in the stomach, throat, foot, teeth) or whatever. It might be easier to say *J'ai mal ici*, it hurts here, and point.

Be prepared to have a thermometer thrust up a sensitive part of your anatomy (normal body temperature in centigrade is 37°). The French place great faith in the anal as opposed to the oral passages. One of their favourite forms of remedy is *le suppositoire*, suppository, prescribed not merely for digestive affliction, as in other countries, but for a whole range of ailments including headaches. This way, a drug that could be difficult to swallow or might upset the stomach is absorbed directly into the body through the bowel.

Une ampoule is another popular package, but much less worrying. It is simply a small glass phial holding a measured dose of medicine and is, of course, very expensive.

At the end of the consultation, the doctor will probably give you *une ordonnance*, prescription, and present his bill. You must pay this in full on the spot; cash is appreciated. Ask for a receipt and keep it, together with any prescriptions, pharmacy and hospital receipts, in order to claim back on the insurance.

Form E111 If you are British and have acquired a form E111 under the reciprocal health agreement with France (see p. 10), you should proceed as follows. Forget the small print and ask the doctor himself, not the welfare office, for a slip known as *une feuille de maladie*. Next, having paid the whole of the doctor's bill, go to the pharmacy with your prescription and the slip. Again, you will be charged the full price for the medicines, while the price label or *vignette* is detached from each one and stuck in the *feuille*. You can use the same slip after any further visits to the doctor.

Finally, you search out the local social security office (*caisse d'assurance primaire* or *bureau de la sécurité sociale*), usually in the nearest large town; the doctor or pharmacist can direct you. There you hand over the *feuille de maladie*, prescriptions and form E111. Make sure the form is returned to you, in case you need it

again. A couple of months later you should receive a
money order at home, refunding three-quarters of your
medical expenses, or more if they were very large.

French dentists — *le* or *la dentiste*, according to sex —   *The dentist*
operate in the same way. All the above concerning
doctors applies to them too.

They are not difficult to locate, though less thick on
the ground than in the USA, where there are twice the
number of dentists per person. Apparently, there are as
many dentists in France as masseurs.

The chances are that you won't have to go near a doctor   *The pharmacy*
anyhow, unless you're struck by a serious accident or
illness. Even if he is a rip-off merchant, the pharmacist
performs a valuable service. He is expert in first aid and
should be your first resort for any minor aches and pains
or injuries. If the problem is beyond his scope, he will
send you to a doctor.

The pharmacist is a qualified dispensing chemist, who
must by law own and run his shop. These days, he is
supplied by the giant pharmaceutical companies and
rarely has to make up his own medicines. But in France
he retains the slight aura of a medieval alchemist. One of
his lesser-known skills, to foreigners at any rate, is the
identification of mushrooms. He has large charts and
life-size models for this purpose. So, if you've picked a
basketful of fungi which you believe might be *chanterelles* or the rare *morilles*, take it to the pharmacist to
make sure.

Drugs and medicines, on or off prescription, are
available only from *la pharmacie*. You won't find them
at *la droguerie*, which sells household goods and toilet
articles like soap and shampoo, nor at *le drug-store*,
which is a fast-food-outlet-cum-boutique. The pharmacy
often has a limited stock of luxury toiletries and beauty
preparations, although you would do better at *la parfumerie* for these; it does not sell films and photographic material.

The sign for the pharmacy is a green cross. There is a
rota in each town for night-time and Sunday opening. If
the shop is closed, look on the door for a notice headed
Pharmacie de Garde or *de Service*, which should give the
address of the nearest open one.

Common maladies you might want to consult the

pharmacist about are *un rhume*, cold, *une toux*, cough, *une angine*, sore throat (not angina), *la grippe*, flu, *un entorse*, sprain, and, self-explanatory, *la constipation* and *la diarhée*. For the latter, you would probably be given *élixir parégorique*, which is tincture of opium flavoured with aniseed.

Pills and tablets are *les comprimés*, ointment is *la pommade*, drops are *les gouttes*. A lot of words, like *antiseptique, aspirine, contraceptif*, are easy to remember and brand names, such as Alka-Seltzer, Kleenex, Tampax, Vaseline, are international. Sticking plaster is *le sparadrap*, a bandage is *une bande*.

Other items which you can purchase at the pharmacy, though they might be cheaper at the supermarket or *droguerie*, include *le dentifrice*, toothpaste, *le savon*, soap, *le shampooing, le papier hygiénique*, toilet paper, *les serviettes hygiéniques*, sanitary towels, *les couches*, nappies or diapers.

All these products are expensive. It's sensible to equip yourself for travel with any drugs that you take regularly, a basic first aid kit and essential toiletries.

Incidentally, don't confuse *les médicaments*, drugs in the medical sense, with *les drogues*, narcotics.

Fire

Dial 18 for the fire service. The service is free, unless it's a hoax call.

Firemen are known as *sapeurs-pompiers*. They seem to be a more cheerful crew than the police and often join in celebrations with gusto and their hoses. On New Year's Eve or la Saint-Sylvestre they may be seen spraying the crowds in the street from the top of an apartment block. Immaculate village fire engines are kept at country stations.

Forest fires are a real hazard in many parts of France, not only in the south where they can break out spontaneously. Notices of the *risque/danger d'incendie*, fire danger, should be respected, which means not even throwing a cigarette butt out of the car.

Brushes with the law

Unless you're a hardened criminal, the most likely offence you could commit while in France would be related to driving (see p. 53).

On the other hand, you might end up the victim of crime. Every summer brings horrifying tales of violence in the south of France, often involving innocent tourists as well as local thugs. You court disaster, it seems, by camping in the wild or sleeping in your car.

You probably won't be drawn into the gangland warfare of Marseille, nor be party to *un crime passionnel*, which continues to be a French speciality. But you should watch out for muggers and pickpockets in Paris, particularly on the Métro. Here bands of kids have perfected the art of snatching valuables and are too young to be prosecuted.

The consulate

If you are arrested, contact the nearest consular representative at once. Although he can't actually intervene in the legal processes, he can protect your interests and ensure that you receive fair treatment.

The consulate is a last ditch. Its role is to help and advise nationals in grave difficulty, on the scale of arrest or a serious accident. It is not a bank, travel agency, employment or social workers' office, missing persons bureau or information centre.

The police

Dial 17 for the police in emergency. Should you require a police station, ask for *le commissariat* (*de police*) or, in the countryside and small towns especially, *la gendarmerie*. *Le préfecture de police* is the Paris police headquarters. For non-urgent phone calls to the police, look them up under any of the headings above (usually it will be *commissariat*) in the pink section at the front of the telephone directory.

The police should be notified of any theft or loss of possessions. You should also report to them first if you lose your passport, then to the nearest consulate or embassy. The police are a source of information and advice as well as law enforcers, and their responsibilities extend to social matters, debts, residence permits and so on. On the other hand, their powers might strike the innocent as somewhat arbitrary. They can apprehend you if you're not carrying any identification; they can charge you with vagrancy if you have less than 10f on you; and they have the right to hold you in custody for 48 hours without charge.

A policeman is known as *un flic* in vulgar parlance. But the polite approach to one in the street is *Pardon, M. l'agent* — Excuse me, officer.

There are two major varieties of police in France — the *agents de police*, organized on a local basis, and the *gendarmes*, recruited nationally. The distinction between them is not of vast moment to the foreigner, who will notice chiefly that there are lots of them, that their general demeanour is grumpy (unlike the British bobby) and that they carry guns. A third type, the CRS (Compagnie Républicaine de Sécurité) have a fearsome image as riot police, somewhat unjustly since they combine this function with mountain rescue, beach safety and motorway patrols.

Lawyers *Un avocat* is a lawyer, barrister, defending counsel (and also an avocado pear); you are unlikely to need one. However, you might require *un notaire*, which can be translated as a public notary; he deals with house sales, contracts, wills and other documents and is roughly equivalent to an English solicitor. *Un huissier* is more than a bailiff, dealing not only with seizure of property and goods, but also summonses, statements, writs and lawsuits; he is called in if there's any dispute over the facts of a road accident.

Finding things out

The syndicat d'initiative (tourist office)

One of the most useful institutions that France has to offer the visitor is *le syndicat d'initiative*, the tourist office, sometimes called *office/bureau de tourisme* instead. It can be found in most French towns and many a village, signposted by the letters *SI*, *OT* or *TSI*, often with a dotted i symbol. It is also marked on the town plans in the Michelin red guide.

The *syndicat* is a mine of free information on hotels, restaurants, camp-sites, sporting facilities, transport, entertainments, local happenings. It dispenses lists and leaflets, maps and plans. The staff vary. They can be extremely helpful and willing to enter into value judgements on, say, the best restaurant in town. Or they will only answer simple queries like when market day is, and react to anything else with a clutch of brochures. English is not always spoken. Most of the *syndicats* are closed for lunch and out of the main holiday season.

Tourist offices displaying an Accueil de France sign specialize in hotel bookings, for personal callers only and for the same night. Many of these are situated at ports, air terminals and main railway stations.

The Paris tourist office doubles as a *comité régional de tourisme*, the overall tourist authority for the region. There are over 20 of these committees throughout

France (addresses from the French Government Tourist Office); they will send detailed information about the region by post but, apart from the one in Paris, are not equipped to deal with phone calls and visitors.

For anything to do with property, *la mairie* is the place. *The mairie*
This is the seat of the mayor who, as both chief elected officer on the municipal council and representative of the state, is the hub of the community. If you're looking for somewhere to rent, the *mairie* is a good source of information. And if you're buying a house, you can inspect plans at the *mairie* and obtain general advice.

The mayor is usually up to date on local gossip and feuding, and he frequently organizes events such as fêtes and mushroom walks. He also presides over civil marriages, the only type recognized by law.

With a *Pardon, Monsieur/Madame* (excuse me, Sir/ *Asking the*
Madam) and *Où est* or *Je cherche* (where is, or I'm *way*
looking for) the church, beach or whatever, asking the way is easy. Understanding the directions can be more tricky. Don't confuse *tout droit*, straight on, with *à droite*, right. *A gauche* is left.

French summer time, in common with the rest of the *The time*
continent, lasts from March to September and is one hour in advance of French winter time. For most of the year, therefore, France is an hour ahead of the UK, and six or seven hours ahead of US eastern standard time.

You're never very far from a town hall or church with a clock on it in France. So you probably won't have to accost anyone with a *Vous avez l'heure, s'il vous plaît?* (what time is it, please?) Some French clocks strike twice, in case you missed it the first time.

In officialese and timetables the French use the 24-hour clock. Thus 7 p.m. is 19h or 19.00 and midnight is 24h or 24.00; 8.30 a.m. is 8h 30 or 08.30. Half an hour is written 1/2h; two and a half hours would be 2h 1/2.

They also refer to the 24-hour clock in speech. So remember to specify *six heures du soir* (6 in the evening) if you don't want to say *dix-huit heures* (18.00).

The French call a week *une semaine* or *huit jours* (8 days). A fortnight is *quinze jours* (15 days). Like other Europeans, but unlike Americans, they write the date in the order day, month, year (not month, day, year). (See also p. 153.)

Not allowed   If your French vocabulary is limited, it can save a great deal of trouble if you know when things are not allowed. Two main words are used to convey the message 'forbidden' — *interdit* or *il est interdit de*, and *défense de* or *il est défendu de*. Hence signs saying *entrée interdite*, no entry, *défense d'afficher*, stick no bills, and so on.

Locating and using the lavatory

French, like other languages, has numerous terms for the lavatory. You can safely ask for, and easily remember, *les toilettes*.

Euphemisms   This word appears on signs. About as common is *WC* or *les WC* (i.e. water closet), pronounced 'lay-vay-say' or 'lay-dubla-vay-say'. Equally, you could be directed to *messieurs*, gentlemen, or *dames*, ladies; or to *les lavabos*, meaning washbasins and probably toilets; or possibly to *les cabinets*. There is also the mysterious 00 sign, which may be connected with the English word loo. In polite conversation, particularly in a French home, you might ask for *le petit coin* (literally, the little room).

Hygiene and privacy   For a nation so concerned with food and drink, the French are strangely unconcerned about eliminating the results. Hotels and private houses often have a sort of unventilated box in the middle of the hall or landing. Plumbing and drainage generally is appalling — but then it all contributes to that uniquely French smell. Segregation can't be relied on and women should be warned that, in a public toilet, they might have to walk past a row of urinating men to reach the only cubicle with a door.

Even in a plush restaurant you might be subjected to the footpad and squatter kind of facility, which must be the most insanitary device ever invented. Basically, it is a hole in the ground with a porcelain surround and slightly raised foothold on either side, but no toilet seat. When you flush it, water inundates everything without much real effect. You have to be athletic to avoid the flood, and to adopt the correct squatting posture in the first place.

Things have improved, nevertheless, in the last ten years or so. Many of the fly-infested footpads have been replaced by the conventional upright type of lavatory, with a corresponding advance in cleanliness. Toilet paper is frequently provided, even if its quality leaves much to be desired. Indeed, some cafés and bars are positively

Reproduced by courtesy of *Punch*

proud to show you to their smart modern toilets, though others maintain the old traditions. You can treat these as public conveniences: just walk into a café and ask and don't feel obliged to buy a drink.

Other public lavatories are to be found at railway and Metro stations, underground garages, and in the street — none to be recommended. Only service stations have a reasonable overall standard. There's sometimes a fixed charge at public toilets, which might be levied by an attendant; or there may be a fierce old lady guarding the toilet paper, who must be tipped,

How do you flush a French lavatory? Look for the small knob on top of the cistern and pull it upwards. Never use the toilet for refuse disposal: it can't cope with anything apart from its allotted role.

You won't see a sign to *le pissoir* or *la pissotière*, the urinal, because it's all too obvious. It's also known as *la vespasienne*, after the Emperor Vespasian who is credited with its introduction in ancient Rome. The public urinal is a feature of every French square and market place, often placed strategically next to the church. Yet this wealth of conveniences has failed to satisfy the Frenchman's urge for *al fresco* relief, preferably at a roadside, as you will soon observe. Hence all those *défense d'uriner* strictures.

*Public
urinals*

The poor Parisian male is losing his 300 *pissoirs* to the *sanisette*. This is the unisex superloo, which first invaded Britain in London's Leicester Square. You insert 1f and are ushered in to music, then escape before an automatic flush and brush of the entire cubicle and a green light beckons the next customer.

Driving

Driving in France is still a delight, even though it's the country with the highest level of car ownership in the EEC. The French have a passion for cars, which goes well with their new national indulgences, holidays and *le weekend*. Foreign models are considered especially chic, and large squashy saloons are more desirable than the cheap and cheerful Citroën 2CV or Renault 4.

Frenchmen are supposed to treat their cars as they treat women. Whatever this means, they like to drive fast and recklessly, using the brakes a lot, speeding away from the lights, overtaking whenever possible. Aggressiveness, impatience, intolerance and other proverbial French characteristics are reflected in their behaviour towards fellow motorists, and it all contributes to the high accident rate. The number of deaths per road-user in France is at least double that of the USA, UK, Sweden or Japan.

However, traffic density is only a problem in Paris and the large towns and on some trunk roads. These can be congested and unpleasant (particularly as there's an all too obvious tendency to compensate for lack of lavatories by using the verges or shoulders). But it's quite easy to avoid main roads. The motorway system is excellent and under-used. France now boasts over 3,000 miles of *autoroute*, radiating from the capital in all directions and providing easy access to most of the important cities and tourist regions. Minor roads are of a good overall standard. The most common imperfections are *chaussée déformée* and *accotements non stabilisés* (bad road surface and soft verges), apparently regarded as natural hazards to be pointed out on signs rather than remedied. But once you're accustomed to stretches of bad surfacing, the occasional pothole, adverse cambers and lack of edging, the driving itself is a pleasure.

You can go for miles along straight poplar-lined roads and encounter scarcely another vehicle, particularly if you travel through the hallowed break between 12 and 2 when every French citizen has stopped for lunch. The wise motorist will also avoid peak holiday periods (see pp. 1 and 3), and will steer clear of towns during rush hours, remembering that there are four of these in France — morning, evening and each side of lunch. Somnolent drivers out for a spin after a heavy meal are a peril of Sunday afternoons.

Preliminaries

What you must take

A full national or state driving licence (not provisional) and the vehicle registration certificate or logbook, known as *une carte grise*, are required. Drivers must be 18 or over. An international permit is not necessary. If the vehicle is not registered in your name, you need a letter of authorization from the owner as well.

An insurance certificate is obligatory, preferably giving fully comprehensive cover. Although third-party cover is now the legal minimum in the EEC, it is advisable to extend this with an international insurance certificate or green card, which any insurance company will supply for a small fee. The authorities recognize a green card at once and are unlikely to query it.

Carry all these documents on you so that you can produce them if requested. The police can ask to see them at any time, as indeed can anyone with whom you are involved in an accident.

An international distinguishing sign for the vehicle, in other words a sticker or plate showing the country of origin, is required.

Seat belts are compulsory for the driver and front seat passenger. Children under ten may not travel in the front, unless the vehicle has no back seat. Seat belts must be worn where fitted, even in the back. Front seat belts are mandatory on all French cars registered after 1 January 1965, and rear seat belts as well on those registered after October 1978.

A red warning triangle in case of breakdown must be carried, unless the car has hazard warning lights. It's sensible to take a triangle anyhow, as the lights might be put out of action.

You must have a complete set of spare lightbulbs.

Headlamp beams should dip to the right. Right-hand-drive cars, therefore, have to be adjusted or fitted with beam converters. These usually make the headlights amber-tinted as well, which is no longer essential, but a good idea if you're sensitive to angry flashing from French drivers.

Additional travel insurance, to cover breakdown and *Wise*
serious repairs, is worth taking out before a motoring *precautions*
trip. In the UK, special policies are offered by the AA
and RAC and organizations like Europ Assistance.
These include cover for various contingencies, such as
providing accommodation while you wait for the car to
be fixed, and could rescue a holiday from disaster.

Get your car serviced before you leave. Make sure too
that you have a kit of basic spare parts — it's not always
easy to remember the French for fan belt when shouting
down a motorway phone. You might add a plastic
temporary windscreen, considering the number of
French road signs devoted to *gravillons*, loose chippings.

If your car is a British make, the spares kit is particularly important. Since most French people buy French,
continental or Japanese cars, there are not many garages
equipped to handle British models. Take a list of dealers
or look them up in the Michelin red guide.

For those with a right-hand-drive car, a nearside wing
or door mirror (which becomes offside in France) makes
all the difference to overtaking. A helpful passenger can
be recommended as well.

To dispel any anxiety about rules of the road, pick up
a *Code de la Route*, the French highway code, from a
French service station.

If you're towing a boat on a trailer or carrying it on a
roof rack, check whether you need to fill in a special
form for customs. At present, canoes, small inflatables
and light sail and motor boats are exempt.

For caravans or campers, see p. 91.

If you're determined to travel during peak periods, and *Traffic*
it can be difficult not to in France, there are several *information*
useful sources of information about traffic conditions.

The Centre National d'Information Routière in Paris
operates a 24-hour service, in French, giving details of
the state of the roads and traffic flow, and suggesting
alternative routes (telephone 858—33—33). Phone
numbers of local centres are given on the Michelin red
maps.

You can also try the Touring Club de France (telephone 532—22—15). For motorways, contact the Centre
des Renseignments des Autoroutes in Paris, open week-
days from 9 a.m. to 7 p.m. (telephone 705—90—01).

The British motoring organizations, the AA and RAC,

have port offices in Calais and Boulogne. The RAC has set up its first roadside bureau in France, at the St-Omer toll booth on the A26.

During the summer, France-Inter on 1829 m broadcasts news bulletins and traffic reports in English, at 9 a.m. and 4 p.m. The BBC provides continental travel news on Radio 4, 1500 m, from May to September.

Rules of the road

Speed limits

Speed limits, unless otherwise indicated, are:

130 km/h (80 mph) on toll motorways
110 km/h (68 mph) on dual carriageways and toll-free motorways
90 km/h (56 mph) on most other roads
60 km/h (37 mph) in built-up areas

Lower limits come into force when the roads are wet. These are 110 km/h on toll motorways, 80 km/h on other roads except in built-up areas.

Speed restrictions are shown by the relevant number of km/h on a round sign. The name of a town or village automatically marks the beginning of a built-up area, and the name with a diagonal red slash through it the end (street lighting has nothing to do with it, unlike British practice). *Rappel*, remember, is to remind you that the speed limit is still in force.

For all drivers within one year of passing their test, the speed limit is 90 km/h — which explains the 90 sign you often see on French cars.

A quick and reasonably accurate way to convert kilometres into miles is to multiply by 6 and subtract the 0; thus 50 km = 30 miles.

Right of way

All roads of any significance, outside built-up areas, are now deemed *passage protégé*, i.e. they have the right of way at junctions with minor roads. The sign for these 'protected' roads is a yellow diamond on a white background. Intersections where you have precedence are marked either by an X sign with the words *passage protégé*, or by a fat arrow crossed by a thin horizontal line.

The yellow diamond with a black bar through it indicates the end of right of way and the commencement of the dreaded *priorité à droite*, priority to the right. This is now largely confined to built-up areas. However, it also applies at points where two equal roads

merge, and in fact anywhere with no signs to the contrary. (It is no longer the rule at roundabouts; see
below.) The principle is simply that you give way to
traffic approaching from the right, in the absence of any
other indication.

So in towns and suburbs, you need to be on your
guard and keep a sharp lookout for side roads joining
your own on the right, from which any vehicle may
suddenly decide to emerge in front of you. At large
junctions or forks of equal-status roads, you must yield
to cars coming from the right. This they can do quite
without warning when another road flows into your own
at an angle from behind. A convergence of three roads is
confusing if you retrace your steps, since the priority
depends on the direction you're travelling in.

Priorité à droite is not difficult, as long as you
remember it, keep a cool head, and watch out for danger
points. Gone are the days, just about, when the French
treated it as a God-given right, to be asserted by tractors
crawling out of farm tracks straight into your path on a
main road — or what felt like one. But you should still
be wary.

Don't forget either that it's not an exclusive preserve
of French nationals. *Priorité à droite* also means that
traffic approaching from your left must give way to you.
Should you meet a French driver grimacing at you, the
chances are that he or she is on your left, waiting for
you to go first.

The French do now provide some indications of who
has precedence. The STOP sign means exactly that — no
cruising gently past it. *Cédez le passage* means give way
or yield. Symbolically, the same message is represented
by an upside-down triangle, often giving the distance to
the intersection, say 100 m.

On all public roads, the police and other emergency
vehicles have priority. This privilege extends to public
services as well, including Electricité, Gaz (gas), Compagnie Générale des Eaux (water).

Bus and taxi lanes are fairly common in towns and
may operate against the flow in a one-way street. They
are identified by a continuous yellow line parallel to the
kerb and you must not, of course, drive in them.

Pedestrian crossings are generally incorporated in
traffic lights at junctions. However, uncontrolled ones
are marked by studs or white stripes across the road.

Once they have stepped onto the crossing, pedestrians are supposed to have right of way over traffic, but it's not advisable to test this out on foot. (For the pedestrian's point of view, see p. 75.)

Roundabouts or traffic circles

As from 1 May 1984, the French have wisely decided that traffic entering a roundabout should give way to traffic already on the roundabout. The *priorité à droite* rule no longer applies here (one wonders how the traffic managed to circulate when it was in force). However, you should be cautious, since French drivers might take time to adapt to the new system. And British motorists should remember that the traffic is going round the 'wrong' way, i.e. anti-clockwise.

Traffic lights

French traffic lights or *feux de circulation* take some getting used to for the British. Like American ones, they change suddenly from red to green, with no alerting amber in between. Much worse is that they are often difficult to see. The French like to suspend them high above the road, the last place a Briton thinks of looking, so that their signal comes across even more faintly. Or else there will be just one traffic light on the right-hand side of the road, which becomes invisible if you get too close to it. In this case, watch the tiny set of lights at eye level on the post.

Some traffic lights have a set of four lights on the right-hand post — red, amber, green and a flashing amber arrow. This last means you can proceed, even though the red light is showing and pedestrians might still be crossing. Many more lights, particularly in towns, have a filter for turning right, with green or amber arrows. Beware of finding yourself in the filter lane, holding up a column of hooting cars, when you want to go straight on. In France, the right-hand lane is fraught with dangers — no haven for timid foreign motorists.

Flashing amber lights in general serve as a warning of something. Flashing red lights indicate a serious obstacle of some kind, and also the fact that a train is approaching at an unguarded level crossing. These crossings are very common in the French countryside and suburbs, with their chilling reminder that *un train peut en cacher un autre*, one train may conceal another.

French policemen sometimes take it upon themselves to direct, or delay, traffic in towns. They do so by means of whistle and gesticulations, perhaps from a podium raised above the exhaust fumes.

A solid single line, yellow or white, in the centre of the road means no overtaking, as does the round sign with two cars next to each other. But you may overtake if there is a broken line along your side of the continuous one.

Overtaking or passing

Overtaking is forbidden in all situations where it would be obvious folly to attempt it, on the brow of a hill, on a corner, at a bus stop and so on. You should not overtake a stationary tram with passengers alighting or descending. Nor are you allowed to exceed 30 km/h (18 mph) when passing funerals, processions and marching troops.

A 2CV in France seems to have hidden powers that enable it to sit on your tail and then surge past. The French love overtaking and will do so at any opportunity, as if they too have some inner compulsion. They make their intentions very clear by coming right up behind you and using the indicators before, during and after. They are severe on slower drivers who get in their way and punctilious about pulling in afterwards — no hogging of the fast lane on dual carriageways.

Lorry drivers tend to be sympathetic to those stuck behind them and will tell you when it's safe to overtake with a wink of the right-hand indicator, followed by a flash of headlights after you're passed. Other forms of flashing can be helpful or ominous, for instance watch out for police. A lone car with headlamps full on usually precedes a slow and heavy load, while a whole line of cars with lights on coming the other way means an accident ahead.

Full-beam or dipped headlights must be used at night and in poor visibility. In built-up areas the headlights should be dipped. Sidelights alone are permitted only when the car is stopped.

Night driving

Sounding the horn at night is forbidden. Instead, you should flash your lights when approaching inter-sections and overtaking. In towns you must never use the horn, day or night, except in real emergencies.

British motorists will miss the cat's eyes on main roads: this great invention has not been adopted in France.

Winter driving Snow chains are a good idea if you're driving to a ski resort. They can be hired from French garages, although probably cheaper in the UK, or bought at a hypermarket. Studded tyres are less practical, unless you're actually staying in a snowbound area. Their use is authorized between 15 November and 15 March on vehicles weighing less than 3,500 kg.

Michelin maps indicate roads that are likely to be snowbound, and give phone numbers for local information on road conditions. You can also ring the road information centre in Paris (858—33—33).

Road signs Many road signs are pictorial, familiar to UK residents and self-explanatory. Written signs, especially those warning of hazards, have a charm all their own (see p. 168 for the most frequent.)

Direction signs Paris is signposted wherever you are in France, which is useful for those who don't know the names of places on the way (unlike the UK, where London exists only within a 40-mile radius). At the other extreme, the most insignificant hamlet may be signposted rather than the town you're heading for, which requires detailed map-reading.

The solution is to be guided by road numbers, normally, but not always, given on signs — rarely given on motorways. Roads are classified into categories: A for *autoroute*, motorway; RN or N for *(route) nationale*, major or very main road; D for *départementale*, secondary or less main road; V for *chemin vicinaux*, minor roads. Some N roads are being downgraded to D, so you may see N and D signs on the same road; the last two digits are usually the same (e.g. N12 = D912).

The French have a sensible arrangement for road signs in all towns, regardless of size. *Toutes directions*, or occasionally *autres directions*, is the route for through traffic, whether it's through a provincial backwater or an urban agglomeration. That way you will get round the town fairly fast, no doubt through its *zone industrielle* (industrial zone), and will almost certainly miss any attractions it has to offer.

Centre ville, town centre, on the other hand, will probably bring you to *son vieux château, ses parcs fleuris* (its old castle, its flower-filled gardens) and all the other things that French towns like to boast of, as well as to the town centre, be it ever so minute. For a small town, *centre ville* is often quicker, unless the square is seized up with a market.

Ignore the *poids lourds*, heavy goods vehicles, signs. These show the recommended route for lorries and usually entail a wider diversion, which is why they can misleadingly signpost somewhere in the opposite direction.

As a road sign, the horizontal arrow is universal and, nine times out of ten, it means straight on, not turn left. Just occasionally, it really does mean go left, which you discover too late when you've shot past the turning. In general, instructions to turn left or right are depicted unambiguously by an arrow branching off from a vertical line.

The alternative route or *itinéraire bis* is a feature of the French holiday scene, and it comes in various guises. *Alternative routes*

A heavy green arrow like a coffin on its side, with Toulouse, Espagne or some faraway place written on the sign, is a suggested holiday route for avoiding main roads. The code is green-on-white for a north—south direction, white-on-green for south—north. It may be longer, but will doubtless be pleasanter.

A yellow arrow on blue shows an *itinéraire de délestage*, which bypasses a bottleneck but is unsuitable for caravans.

You will find roads mysteriously labelled *bison futé*, which might be translated as crafty buffalo. *Bison futé* was dreamt up by the French ministry of transport and is a Red Indian who knows when palefaces are on the warpath. In other words, he recommends officially approved diversions for peak periods. A map covering these alternative routes, *la carte de bison futé*, is free from filling stations.

For the British, Australians, Japanese and others, the most crucial rule of the road in France is that you drive on the right. This leads to unnatural practices like overtaking on the left and circling roundabouts the wrong way, both needing extra care. Overtaking, if in a right-hand-drive car, is much easier with a wing mirror and a cooperative passenger; remember to hold back from the vehicle in front for a clearer view of the road ahead. **Driving on the 'wrong' side**

Roundabout procedure has already been described.

But beware of those mini-roundabouts and islands where a minor road crosses a major one, often a dual carriageway. Here you have to reverse the normal instincts and look first left, then right half-way over — it's the second part which is awkward. Turning left also demands more concentration, since it involves crossing the line of approaching traffic.

One quickly adapts to driving on the right. It has a continental chic and, after the first successful negotiations of the road, you feel that you've arrived, rather like dreaming in French. But don't be deluded: it's all too easy to forget to *serrer à droite* (keep right), particularly when starting up in a country lane after a good picnic.

Filling stations

Une station-service supplies petrol or gas, *un garage* carries out repairs. Many of the filling stations are manned or, in the country, womanned; for, even in this sphere of modern life, the French still prefer the old-fashioned courtesies to the anonymity of self-service. There are, of course, some self-service stations, *libre service* or *servez-vous*. But an attendant may still hover, unable to resist cleaning your windscreen.

Essence, petrol, gas, is sold by the litre and comes in two grades: *essence/ordinaire/normale*, 2 star/standard/regular; *super (carburant)*, 3 star and above/premium/super. Diesel is *gas-oil*. Beware of *petrole* — paraffin.

The simplest and most practical formula is to ask for a full tank — *faites le plein, s'il vous plaît*. Otherwise, you can request so many francs' worth, or so many litres, for example, *pour 220f de super*, or *9 litres d'ordinaire*.

At most places, they will be happy to check the oil or tyres if you say *vérifiez l'huile/les pneus, s'il vous plaît*. Tips are not expected but won't be rejected.

Filling stations usually have toilet facilities (reliable standards at Total) and often shops selling soft drinks, maps, motoring accessories. An increasing number accept credit cards. In rural parts they may close for lunch. Many are closed on Sundays. There are a few 24-hour automatic pumps which take bank notes, usually outside hypermarkets.

Emergencies

Breakdowns

The best car to break down in is a Citroën 2CV or, failing that, a popular French model. Your friendly BL or Ford dealer is not just around the corner in France.

However, a village *mècanicien* (mechanic) will frequently do minor repairs for a modest sum. Something like a loose exhaust, a regular occurrence with French road surfaces, might be fixed for less than 10f.

The operative words are *en panne*, broken down. *Ma voiture est en panne*, my car has broken down, covers a multitude of faults, including running out of petrol, *en panne d'essence*. Naturally, it's helpful to know the French for distributor or clutch, but almost anything can be referred to as *le machin* or *le truc*, the contraption, the what's it, a sort of password which is instantly appreciated. *Ceci ne marche pas*, this isn't working, will take you a long way too.

Garages are obliged to display a list of their charges. Invoices must be fully itemized and replaced parts returned to the customer. Keep everything if you want to put in an insurance claim. *Le garage* may advertise itself according to its speciality, such as *dèpannage*, car repairs; *carrosserie/tolerie*, bodywork; *pose de pare-brise*, windscreens fitted; *remorquage*, towing.

When you break down on the open road, extract the warning triangle from under the suitcases and place it 30 metres behind the car. Alternatively, switch on the hazard warning lights. The next step depends on where you've ended up. You may be lucky enough to see a sign and phone for the Touring Club de France (TCF), which provides a breakdown and general information service. If you can find an ordinary telephone, there is a choice: either dial 6969 for Touring Secours, or 17 for the police, or look up the nearest garage in the Michelin red guide or phone book.

You pay for the assistance, in whatever form it arrives. But the TCF has reciprocal arrangements with motoring organizations in other countries whose members may get a discount.

For what to do in a motorway emergency, see p. 55.

Accidents

If you have an accident, and assuming you're still capable, you must notify the police. But first you should take precautions on the spot: alert other drivers with the warning triangle and/or hazard lights; make a note of the registration number of the other vehicles involved; and try to get the names and addresses of any witnesses. Lock your car if you have to leave it.

Then, preferably accompanied by the other driver,

find the nearest telephone, put in money and dial 17. This is the emergency number, from any phone, for both the police and ambulance (known as SAMU, Service d'Aide Médicale d'Urgence).

The police will produce *un constat*, accident statement form, which must be completed and signed by all parties to the accident, however minor. Keep everything which can be used as evidence in an insurance claim.

With luck, that should be the end of the formalities. However, if there's a disagreement and any party refuses to sign the form, matters get more complicated. The case must be referred to a bailiff who, for a fee, will prepare an independent assessment or *un constat d'hussier*. The police will also make a report, known as *un procès-verbal*. They may even require a surety to cover potential court costs and fines. All this could take several days and, although you'd probably be allowed to proceed on your way, you would be well advised not to enter into a dispute and to avoid becoming embroiled in the French legal system.

Reproduced by courtesy of the artist

In 1982 there were more than 5 million road accidents in France, an average of 35 dead and 900 injured every day. During the holiday rush, with something like 10 million cars on the roads, the accident rate is even higher.

The French have at last admitted the connection between their horrendous accident figures and their high level of alcohol consumption. Posters everywhere point out the dire consequences of drinking and driving. *Driving offences*

The law is similar to that in Britain, which means that half a bottle of wine with a meal is safe, but no more. The legal limit is 80 milligrammes per 100 millilitres of alcohol in the blood. *L'alcootest*, the breathalyser, can be administered at random, although in practice people are usually stopped for some other misdemeanour like speeding. Penalties are severe, ranging from a current minimum fine of 1,200f to imprisonment.

Many French drivers remain undeterred by the numerous radar traps. The latest device for catching would-be speeders is to stamp your toll card with the time you get onto the motorway; the police can check it when you leave to see how fast you've travelled between the two toll booths. The minimum fine for speeding is 600f at present.

Speeding, drinking and other offences are liable to heavy fines or *amendes forfaitaires*, and these must be paid in cash on the spot. Always ask for an official receipt.

You need not pay if you believe yourself innocent and want to take the affair to court; but it is wiser to do so and settle the matter, however aggrieved you might feel. Otherwise the police could demand a deposit against costs and even confiscate your car as a guarantee. You would be in for lengthy and expensive legal proceedings.

People, French and foreign, grumble about the cost of the *autoroutes*. Indeed many lorry drivers save money by using ordinary roads instead, which makes something like the N7, from Paris to the south, as nightmarish as it ever was. **Motorways**

Yet French motorways are magnificent, beautifully landscaped with hills and curves and planted with trees and shrubs. Picture signs are thoughtfully placed to inform you about an interesting feature as you whizz past — a river, forest, château, spectacular view, fruit and vegetables grown locally. The network is constantly expanding. Calais is now within nine miles of the A26, which links with the A1 to Paris. The *autoroutes* even have evocative names, like L'Aquitaine for the A10, La Provençale for the A8, and the famous Autoroute du Soleil for the A6. Roadworks are rare (which will be a relief to British motorists resigned to crawling up the M1 in a single lane), although when they do occur you can get stuck for hours.

Motorway driving   However, French motorways can be quite exacting for the driver. Many of them are 4- rather than 6-lane highways, which results in a marked difference of speed between slow and fast lanes. On hills, they expand to an extra crawler lane for *véhicules lents*, slow vehicles. Overtaking technique is particularly important and it makes sense, when driving at speed, to keep a safe distance between you and the vehicle in front. Driving for long periods in the outer left-hand lane is prohibited, and so are reversing, stopping and U turns.

Feeder roads are often far apart. It's worth checking your intended exit or entrance in advance from the map; make sure it really is an interchange and not just a road going over the motorway. Toll cards also show the interchanges.

Signposting is very clear, with the names of the towns in large letters, though rarely the road number. It helps to know your compass directions, both which way you are actually travelling and the French translation; the distinction between *est*, east, and *ouest*, west, is critical. *Sortie d'autoroute* marks a motorway exit. *Fin d'autoroute* means the end of the motorway and its regulations.

Tolls   The majority of French motorways are toll roads or *autoroutes à péage*. The cost of the toll is based on the distance travelled and type of vehicle. You can work it out eventually from the toll card — a suitable pastime for passengers. Basically, most people will fall into one of two categories — either category 1, for an ordinary car; or category 2, for a car with trailer or caravan, or a camper van. If you disagree with the way you are classified, it's worth arguing.

Since many of the motorways are financed by private enterprise, there is no fixed rate and the tolls vary, though they are likely to be standardized in future. At the moment, the price per kilometre is about 17 centimes, but short spans can be more expensive. You should allow at least 50f to get from Calais to Paris, 150f from Paris to Marseille, and more with a caravan.

The normal practice is to pick up a toll card on entering the motorway and to pay on leaving. However, some motorways levy a flat charge at the beginning. Others have collecting machines where you throw in the right money, *jet de pièces*, shown on a screen, and it's automatically gobbled up.

Services

Everything is designed to distract from the monotony of motorway driving. Services of some kind are found at 10 km intervals, denoted by the familiar symbols — petrol pump, knife and fork, cup, bed. The capital P in a circle means a rest area or *aire de repos*, which provides parking and leg-stretching space, toilets and frequently a picnic spot, furnished with rustic tables and benches, since all self-respecting French people have to sit down in the approved manner to lunch.

Petrol stations, open 24 hours a day, occur about every 20 km. They are generally combined with a buffet or restaurant, sometimes a shop and tourist information bureau (indicated by a dotted i) and occasionally a motel. Some service areas have hotel reservation and foreign exchange facilities as well. There are always public telephones and toilets, as there are also at the toll booths. Toilets, as always in France, are of variable quality. But seasoned travellers tend to rate the service stations more highly than the rest areas in this respect. Details of services are often shown on toll cards.

Self-service-style eating, otherwise rare in France, has intruded on the *autoroutes*. But it's a far cry from the British experience of the motorway café. Whether you want a quick snack or a proper meal attended by waiters, the overall standard of food and drink is good, though expensive. Even the automatic vending machines at filling stations dispense genuine hot coffee and chocolate.

Emergencies

The first thing to do if you break down on the motorway is to get the car off the road and on to the hard shoulder. Prop open the bonnet or hood and put the lights on to make your plight more visible, or place the warning triangle 100 metres behind the car, on the hard

shoulder. Don't, whatever you do, walk on the motorway
or cross it.

Free telephones, connected direct to breakdown and
emergency services, are placed every 2 km along the
motorway. Little signs along the roadside point to the
nearest one. They are on orange posts, with instructions
for use in several languages. But you will need some
basic French to say whether you are simply *en panne*,
broken down, or have had *un accident*, an accident, to
explain the position of your car (before or after the
phone) and to give its registration number.

Garages have to be licenced for motorway work.
There are standard rates for emergency repairs, which
you should ask to see. Minor jobs taking less than half an
hour are done on the spot; for more serious repairs, you
will have to fork out the additional sum for being towed
to a garage, *remorquage*, again at an official price.

The Boulevard
Périphérique

The Boulevard Périphérique is not for those of a nervous
disposition. This motorway ring road encircling Paris,
eight lanes wide in parts, is like a mad perpetual merry-
go-round, jam-packed with cars, vans and lorries all
exceeding the speed limit. But it does enable you to skirt
the capital with its still unresolved traffic problems, and
connects to the motorways converging from north,
south, east and west. It is also toll-free.

To survive the Périphérique calls for bravado. It's no
use hugging the inner lane, because this has a disconcerting
habit of turning into an exit road to some desolate
suburb. You must drive decisively and know exactly
where you're going. Fix your mind on a large destination
and ignore the confusing mass of local signs, particularly
those to the district of Boulogne-Billancourt and the
Bois de Boulogne, which can cause momentary panic if
you're aiming for the Channel ferry.

The signs to look for are Lille, Bruxelles| for the A1;
Metz, Nancy, Strasbourg for the A4; Lyon for the A6;
Chartres, Orléans for the A10/11; Rouen for the A13.
If you are arriving from Calais or Boulogne on the A1,
take the B3 crossover, signposted Paris Est, then Paris
Sud, for all destinations to the south, the Loire valley
and Brittany. Follow the Paris Centre and Paris Ouest
signs for Paris itself and Rouen.

It helps to know your *portes* or gateways, the name
for the main exits from Paris. These are always sign-

posted, whereas road numbers are barely mentioned. A sign above the right-hand lane indicates the next *porte* (e.g. Porte d'Orléans) and, if that's the one you want, you should move into this lane immediately after passing the previous *porte*.

Perusal of the map before tackling the Périphérique is highly recommended. Michelin map no. 101, covering the Paris region, is the best one for the purpose.

Parking

Same word, slightly different meaning. *Le parking* is a car park, parking lot, also known as *un parc de stationnement*. *Stationnement* is parking or waiting.

In most towns of any size, parking is controlled by the blue zone system. Once within the *zone bleue*, which is clearly announced on signs, you are allowed to park for a limited period, usually 1 hour to 1½ hours. You must also display *un disque de contrôle* showing the time when you parked the car. These discs are available free from a tourist office, tobacconist, police station or customs office and are valid in any town with a blue zone (but as a foreigner it's quite possible to manage without). The *zone bleue* is in force between the hours of 9 a.m. and 12.30 p.m. and 2.30 and 7 p.m., except on Sundays and public holidays.

In large towns there may be parking meters, operating between 9 a.m. and 7 p.m. Sometimes they issue a ticket, which should be displayed on the car.

In small towns and villages, parking is restricted to certain days or weeks. A sign saying *stationnement jours impairs* means that parking is permitted only on odd dates of the month (i.e. 1, 3, 5, 7 etc.); *jours pairs* means even dates.

Stationnement interdit means no parking, accompanied by a symbolic P in a circle with a line through it. Parking is prohibited where the kerb is marked with red dashes, and anywhere else that would cause a hazard or obstruction. Illegally parked vehicles may be towed away and recovery is expensive.

At night offside parking lights are compulsory wherever there are no street lights.

Parking in Paris

Don't, if you can help it. With roughly one million private cars owned by Parisians, traffic congestion in the capital is horrendous. The parking problem has still not been resolved, simply because there are more cars than there is space for them.

Many city dwellers have given up the struggle and keep their cars outside central Paris. But the authorities in Paris and the surrounding *départements* have countered with a law against leaving a vehicle in the same place on any public road for more than 24 hours at a stretch.

The centre of Paris is now a *zone grise*, grey zone, with parking meters supervised by traffic wardens in blue uniforms. The meters take 1f and 50c coins and cost about 4f an hour. More than 30 large underground car parks have been built since the 1960s, where parking is slightly cheaper. Other districts are *zone bleue*.

Penalties for infringement of the parking regulations are strictly enforced and fines are steep. Such measures, together with improvements in public transport (see p. 67), have relieved some of the pressure, but can do no more as long as the French continue to be crazy about cars and the capital remains overpopulated.

Maps and guides

Foreign drivers in France tend to fall into two categories: there is the speed merchant, rushing down the motorways to the south and refusing to stop for anything but fuel; and the dawdler who keeps to the D and V roads and is willingly deflected at every turn. There is also a hybrid, the person who alternates judicious motorway dashes with carefree meandering. Whichever camp you belong to, good maps are vital — as is knowing how to use them to full advantage.

Michelin

The Michelin library is indispensable, having the added merit that all its maps and guides cross-refer and tie up together. For basic route planning and reaching a destination, the red map covers the whole country at a scale of 1 cm : 10 km. It can be bought as a single sheet (no. 989), a reversible sheet (no. 916), or split for north (no. 998) and south (no. 999). As well as major roads and motorways, it picks out certain D roads in yellow as less crowded.

For local touring once you've arrived, the yellow maps are the key. France is covered by 37 of these, at a scale of 1 cm : 2 km. On the same scale, Michelin have produced several larger maps which conveniently embrace whole regions, such as Brittany and Alsace.

The yellow maps give a comprehensive picture of an

area, plus a little bit more to heighten the pleasure of exploration. Picturesque routes are shaded green, while arrows indicate steep roads; there are symbols for fine views, for sporting activities, indeed for anything from a windmill to 'another curiosity' (*autre curiosité*); paths for cyclists and ramblers are given, and ferries for cars; places mentioned in the Michelin red guide are underlined in red; and towns which have a plan in the same guide are identified with a rectangle.

Start the other way round, with the red guide to hotels and restaurants, look up a town, and you will be directed to the appropriate yellow map. Under Clermont-Ferrand, for instance, will be found 74 ⑭ , which means it can be located on map no. 73, fold 14.

The red guide is not only a bible of bodily comforts but, in effect, a map of urban France. Detailed town plans show all the important features, facilities and places of interest, with reference numbers for main routes repeated on the corresponding yellow map. Under the town entries are included population figures, altitude, postal and telephone codes and other useful information. Although published in French, the red guide contains an introduction in English and other languages, which explains how to use the book and the meaning of the symbols.

The Michelin green guides to the regions elaborate on the star-rated sights briefly alluded to in the red guide. They too contain town plans, on the same basis and numbering system but more detailed. They also supply maps for some of the smaller places not illustrated in the red guide. Naturally, the yellow maps are complementary to the green guides as well. An increasing number of the green guides are available in English translation.

There is nothing to rival the Michelin collection as a whole (they also publish an annual guide, *Camping Caravaning France*), although numerous competitors exist.

The Institut Géographique National (IGN) have two sets *Others* of tourist maps or *cartes touristiques* useful to motorists, in addition to their more specialized maps for walkers and others (see p. 76). These are the *série rouge*, red cover, which 'does' France in 15 sheets at a scale of 1 cm : 2.5 km and pin-points areas of particular interest;

and the *série verte*, green cover, in 73 sheets at 1 cm :
1 km.

Indexed plans to 123 towns can be obtained from
Plans-Guides Blay. Other map publishers worth mention-
ing are Recta, Hallwag, Philips and Kummerley & Frey.

Paris   For Paris there are three helpful maps from Michelin —
the suburbs and Boulevard Périphérique, no. 101, scale
1 cm : 0.5 km; environs of Paris, no. 96, scale 1 cm :
1 km; and the surrounding region as far as Rouen and
Troyes, no. 97, scale 1 cm : 2 km. (For other maps and
guides to the capital, see p. 139).

Importing a car   If your car is registered in the UK, it need not be re-
from the UK   registered in France for another year. After 12 months'
residence, you become eligible for a French driving
licence without having to take a test.

A car can be temporarily imported, which means
without additional customs documents, for up to six
months in any one year. For a longer period or perma-
nently, you should inquire about the rules.

The car must be insured, either in Britain or France,
which is more expensive. French road tax, on the other
hand, decreases the older and less powerful the vehicle.
You can buy the car tax sticker or *vignette* at the
tobacconists'.

For motorbikes and car rental, see pp. 73 and 74.

Getting About – from Trains to Two Feet

The TGV (Train à Grande Vitesse), the swiftest train in the world, is a fitting flagship for the highly efficient French railways. The state-owned SNCF (Société Nationale des Chemins de Fer Français) reaches over 6,000 destinations and maintains a reputation for safety and punctuality. Its long-distance trains are the ultimate in comfort and speed. Averaging around 90 mph, the famous 'Mistral' to Marseille, the 'Capitole' to Toulouse and the 'Aquitaine' to Bordeaux were the fastest in Europe, until the advent of the high-speed baby. As well as this, SNCF has developed turbotrains, equipped with gas turbine engines, and the luxury Corail carriages, with air conditioning, automatic doors and individual airline-type seats.

Although Paris is still the focal point of the rail network, inter-regional connections have improved enormously. Today you can journey direct between Nice and Bordeaux in ten hours. Cross-country routes link relatively insignificant places as well, not just major cities.

SNCF operations cover a wide field. Over 200 stations offer car rental and bicycle hire, known as Train + Auto and Train + Vélo. Train + Hotel is for booking accommodation. Bus services, tourist coaches, boat cruises and package holidays are all organized by SNCF.

On the trains themselves, there is a wide range of facilities. Trains-Auto-Couchettes tranport cars and motorbikes and their owners. Unaccompanied children can be put in the charge of a hostess, through the Jeune Voyageur Service (JVS), and some trains have special family compartments.

You can travel light by registering your baggage, including skis and cycles, so that it is carried separately. SNCF will even collect and deliver to your home or hotel. At most stations, there are left-luggage offices or *consignes* and baggage trolleys for the use of passengers.

Information   A useful booklet, *Le Guide pratique du voyageur*, gives details of SNCF services and fares. It is free at stations.

Types of train   There are several varieties of train in France, some with deceptive names. The *autorail*, far from implying velocity, is one of the slowest, often a sort of bus on rails. This and the *omnibus*, stopping at every station, are usually second-class only.

The *direct* is a through train and probably *un express*, too, halting only at large stations. *Un rapide* means what it says and is the most 'express' of all.

The TGV, which is capable of a record-breaking 380 km/h (237 mph), attains a speed of 260 km/h (162 mph) between Paris and Lyon. To date, it connects Paris with Dijon, Besançon, Lyon, Geneva, Montpellier and Marseille. The journey time between Paris and Lyon has been reduced from nearly four hours to two. New track has been built for this stretch, and the space-age station of Le Creusot has arisen in the middle of an industrial no man's land. It's an experience just to watch the TGV gliding up the platform, on the dot, like some magnificent sharp-nosed monster. A second high-speed railway is to run between Paris and Bordeaux.

Sleeping and   Couchettes are provided on all night trains. These are
eating   four berths per compartment in first class, six in second. They are non-smoking, but ashtrays, plus shaving points and mirrors, are distributed along the corridors.

Voitures-lits, sleeping cars, on most main lines, generally bear the TEN (Trans Euro Nuit) emblem. These are grander, with washbasins and room service, single or double in first class, two- or three-bedded in second. Reservations are obligatory for all sleeping accommodation on trains.

Perhaps it is to their credit that the French have not mastered the art of snacks. The *minibar*, a trolley which is wheeled up and down almost every train, stocks an unimaginative selection of refreshments — *le sandwich*, French version (half a dry *baguette*, or bread roll, with a slice of ham), cans of beer, and coffee, often already sweetened. Everything is expensive: a small bottle of mineral water will set you back 7f or so. The *bar-buffet* carriage, on fast trains, extends to warmed-up pizzas, cellophane-wrapped cake, aperitifs and wines.

Sometimes there is a cafeteria-type *gril-express* and

maybe a *wagon-restaurant* with waiters. Timetables indicate what you can expect. On TGV and Corail trains, first-class passengers can order tray meals at their seats; these should be reserved ahead.

Train toilets are nasty on the whole, not through any fault of their own, but because of travellers' habits.

British visitors will be pleasantly surprised by the comparatively low cost of train fares in France. Moreover, apart from the deals reserved for foreigners like France Vacances and the Eurail Pass (see p. 14), numerous discounts can be obtained in France.

Fares and supplements

Un billet-séjour, holiday return, for example, allows a 25 per cent reduction on the normal fare, as does the *billet mini-groupes* for five people together. A *carte couple* entitles one of a married couple to go at half price, when travelling off peak with his or her spouse. It is valid for five years and you don't need to be French or a permanent resident to benefit. In fact, you don't have to be married, as long as you can produce *un certificat de concubinage* to prove that you're living together. (France can be recommended for free love: since the 1970s, the law has granted virtually the same rights to the married and unmarried couple; illegitimacy no longer has a stigma either.)

La carte famille is a similar offer for families. The *carte jeune*, for those aged 12 to 25, enables the holder to travel at half price. *Un abonnement* or season ticket can be equally advantageous.

These fares and deals apply to the TGV, too, except during peak hours when a supplement is /payable..

Watch out for other supplements to the basic fare. They are levied on the TEE (Trans Europ Express) trains, which are first-class only, and on some *rapides* and *intercité* trains. You can buy a *carnet* or book of 15 supplement coupons to meet such eventualities.

Reservations are compulsory for the TGV, both first and second class, on the principle that it admits only as many passengers as there are seats. The system is computerized.

TGV reservations

You may purchase your ticket and reserve a seat in advance, up to two months before. Or you can do so at the station in the ordinary way, at the time of the journey; bookings are accepted until a few minutes before departure.

Alternatively, if you already have a ticket but no reservation, you can make one through the automatic machine on the platform, called TGV Réservation Rapide. This will book you on to the first train with seats available leaving within the hour.

Stations   Indifferent signposting frequently hinders the search for the station, or *la gare*. It's advisable to use a Michelin map or town plan for guidance.

Only the French could associate stations with gastronomic excellence. In Paris, the Gare de Lyon restaurant is celebrated for such dishes as *quenelles de brochet* and classified a historic monument for its period décor. The restaurant or *buffet de gare* in many a humbler station attracts regular custom from the locals as well as travellers. Perhaps this helps explain why the food is generally so poor on the trains themselves.

Billets is the sign for the ticket office. You should ask for *un aller*, single, or *aller-retour*, return (round-trip), in *première* or *deuxième classe* (first or second class). Credit cards are usually accepted. *Locations* is the sign for advance reservations, *Renseignements* for information. Timetables or *horaires* are displayed on boards and freely supplied as booklets. Verbal sources seem incapable of agreeing on the precise time of a French train, so it's wise to check and double-check.

At the platform entrance where it says *Accès aux quais* (entrance to platforms), stands an orange pillar, the most vital element of a French station. This is the 'composting' machine, which has replaced human ticket control. Simply follow the instructions to *Compostez-le* (date-stamp it) by inserting your ticket in the slot; it emerges stamped with the date, and thus made valid for travel. If you have put the ticket in upside down, the machine will light up with the words *Tournez votre ticket*, turn your ticket over. This procedure is only necessary for tickets bought inside France, not for those acquired abroad.

Failure to validate a ticket incurs a fine of 20 per cent on top of the fare (a minimum of 34f). The trains are rife with inspectors, presumably redundant ticket collectors, so it is essential to *composter*. If you break your journey and resume it on the same day, there is no need to validate the ticket again, but you must do so after an overnight stop.

Platforms or *quais* are not always clearly numbered, and you have to look carefully. Tracks or lines (*voies*) are often numbered as well, which can be confusing. The *sortie* or exit is usually through a tunnel under the tracks, although in minor stations it may just be a matter of walking across the line. This is disturbing if you get out of the wrong side of the train and are forced to wait for it to pull out of the station before you can join anxious loved ones at the barrier.

A plan of the *composition des trains* on the platform shows where first- and second-class compartments will fall when the train arrives. The destination of a train is written on the outside of the carriages. Except for the TGV, it's quite a climb up the steps to get into the carriage.

Planes

Air Inter, the French domestic airline, has one of the most comprehensive networks in Europe and serves over 30 destinations throughout France. Its particular value, in a country which is still so capital-orientated, is the fact that it links the regions with each other and not merely with Paris. It also connects with many Air France international flights to Paris.

Airports

The Paris airports or *aéroports* are Roissy-Charles de Gaulle, chiefly international flights, and Orly, mainly domestic and charter (see p. 70). Many other airports are dignified by their own names — Mérignac for Bordeaux, Blagnac for Toulouse, Marignane for Marseille. One of the most important, Lyon Satolas, is impressively organized for businessmen and skiers. Nice is another major airport, despite its alarming perch on the edge of the sea, and is served by the new 'airbus'.

An *aérogare* is the air terminal and *correspondances* are connecting flights.

Cheap fares

Anyone with a foreign passport can claim 25 per cent off normal fares. Numerous categories qualify for discounts on designated flights, among them children, young people, students, families, senior citizens, groups. Frequent users can save about a third with a season ticket, while holders of an SNCF *abonnement* or season ticket are entitled to a reduction. Round-trip tickets also work out cheaper.

Buses Buses are not much in evidence in France (except in Paris; see below) and one might almost think they were despised as a form of transport. After all, most people are independently motorized, either with a car, motor-bike or moped, and the trains represent a cheap and efficient alternative. There is nothing on a national scale to compare with the American Greyhound or British National Express; indeed, many of the long-distance services are operated from abroad (see p. 15).

Nevertheless, local buses do exist. The best place to find out about them is the tourist office or the railway station. They are often run by SNCF, who also organize excursions in coaches (*autocars* or *cars*).

Most buses stop running about 8.30 or 9 in the evening. In the countryside, *l'autobus* or bus might make one journey two or three times a week, usually on market days, going out in the early morning and returning in the evening. In some towns, the 'bus' may turn out to be an old-fashioned tram or trolley bus.

La gare d'autobus is the bus station and *un arrêt d'autobus* a bus stop. Queuing is unheard-of. You should signal to stop the bus. Get in at the door marked *montée* and leave the vehicle by the *sortie*, exit. No smoking is the general rule.

Taxis Taxis are easily identified by that self-same international word on the roof of the car. They are only allowed to pick up from a cab rank (*station de taxi* or *tête de station*), often situated outside the railway station. Or you can summon a cab by phone: look under taxi in the local directory.

The fare is shown on the meter (check that there is one before you get in), together with any supplements for baggage and so on. You should add 15 per cent as a tip. There is often a fixed charge for certain routes, like the airport to the centre of town. Don't be surprised to see the driver alter the meter at night, when a slightly higher rate comes into force. Always inquire about the price first for a long trip; you might have to pay for the return trip if your journey takes you out of town.

Beware of the meterless cabs that lurk near big hotels and stations. These do not have the taxi sign on the roof, are not licensed and can charge what they like — as much as possible in the case of gullible tourists. If you do hire one, agree on the price before committing yourself. The same goes for chauffeur-driven cars, which may be hired on a trip or time basis. English-speaking drivers are often available in Paris.

Public transport in Paris

If Paris is still one of the most congested capitals in the world, it has at least solved the problem of public transport. The system, consisting of Métro and RER trains and the buses, is fast and efficient. It is well integrated: tickets are interchangeable on all three and most bus routes terminate near a station. Above all, it is cheap, thanks to heavy subsidies, and this alone has ensured its success.

The body responsible for public transport in the city is the RATP (Régie Autonome des Transports Parisiens). It has numerous offices throughout Paris.

The visitor might be tempted to buy *un billet de tourisme*, a pass giving unlimited travel on the Métro, RER and buses for a period of two, four or seven days. It is obtainable, on production of a passport, from RATP offices and main Métro and SNCF stations, or in advance from the French Government Tourist Office. *La carte orange* is a similar monthly pass.

But be careful: Paris is one of the best cities for walking in and the *billet de tourisme* won't actually save you money unless you make extensive use of public transport. It could easily work out more expensive than buying ordinary *carnets* (see below).

For maps and guides to Paris, see p. 139.

The Métro

In Paris you are never further than 500 metres from an underground or subway station. The Métro (or Métropolitain) dates from the turn of the century, but it has been thoroughly updated. Gone is its humble image, the reek of sweat and garlic; disappearing are the rattly wooden carriages, the antique lifts and some of the period charm of the original stations.

Smooth new trains on rubber tyres are fast and frequent, running steadily from 5.30 a.m. to 1 a.m. They are clean, with smoking banned throughout. Escalators and moving pavements, automatic ticket barriers and electronic route maps have been installed at most stations. Others have been redecorated: the stop for the Louvre is almost an art gallery in its own right.

There is a flat fare for the Métro. In other words, one ticket allows you to go anywhere within the system.

Billets, also known as *tickets* in French, may be purchased singly, or in a *carnet*, book, of ten, which is cheaper. Tickets are sold at stations, bus termini, tobacconists and RATP offices.

There is no point buying a first-class ticket, unless you plan to use the Métro at the same time as everyone else. First-class travel is being phased out by the socialist government, and at most times of day you can sit in a first- or second-class carriage regardless of your ticket. The distinction between first and second class now operates only during the rush hour, when you must have the appropriate ticket.

Ticket control is automated at all stations. You simply slot your ticket into a machine to gain access to the platform. However, you must hang on to the ticket as inspectors are common.

The lines of the Métro are distinguished by numbers, but more often referred to by the names of the stations that terminate each line. Remembering these end stations or *directions* is the key to Métro travel. You should follow the illuminated orange signs for the *direction* you need. When you have to change trains, the appropriate exit for your *correspondance*, connection, is similarly indicated. It may be a very long walk.

Métro maps are displayed at all stations. Some are electric route planners, which work out your journey at the touch of a button. If hopelessly bewildered, you might be able to ask the *chef de station*, station master, who lurks in a glass booth on some platforms at some stations.

Doors close automatically on the trains, but you must release a catch in the middle to open them. As on the buses, there are a number of seats reserved for the disabled, known as *mutilés*, elderly or pregnant, who have the right to expel you if you are none of these.

The RER   RER stands for Réseau Express Régional. This is the recent extension to the Métro, which reaches to the suburbs and beyond and across Paris.

To the average visitor, its chief value lies in linking Charles de Gaulle airport and the Gare du Nord (one of the Paris main line stations), and the Gare du Nord with Gare de Lyon (another); with fewer intermediate stations, it is quicker than the Métro. The RER also links with the SNCF railway between Les Invalides and Ver-

'He's right, you know: a field amputation of a nether limb takes precedence over an eight-month unwanted pregnancy.'

Reproduced by courtesy of *Punch*

sailles, and it goes out as far as St-Germain-en-Laye, with its Renaissance château and park, via the new town of La Défense.

Outside the city limits, the RER operates a separate ticket system, where fares depend on distance. However, within the Ville de Paris ordinary Métro tickets are acceptable on the RER. It is doubly important to retain your ticket when using both systems, so that you can change from one to the other. In the case of the RER, you have to present your ticket to a machine on leaving. If you have finished your journey, it will say *Passez*, proceed, and keep the ticket; if not, it will tell you to *Prenez votre ticket*, take your ticket, and spit it back at you, enabling you to continue on the Métro.

Buses

With over 70 miles of traffic-free bus lanes in Paris, the bus is now an efficient, as well as interesting, mode of transport. Services are frequent and times are shown at most bus stops. All buses run between 7 a.m. and 8.30 p.m., but services are generally sparser than on the Métro, especially in the evenings and on Sundays and holidays. Travel by bus also works out more expensive than the Métro with its flat fare system.

Second-class Métro tickets are used for the buses and bought in the same way (see above under Métro). You can buy a single ticket on the bus itself, but this is more expensive.

One ticket is valid for a journey up to two *sections* or fare stages. These are marked *fin de section*, end of stage, at the bus stop and on the route diagrams so you will see clearly how many you need for your journey. Two tickets are required for longer trips or if you change buses, and you will need four to go out to the suburbs.

The bus stop is a post on the pavement with red and yellow panels, and the name of the street or corner. The same names appear on the route maps, which makes it easy to find your way around. Buses also bear the destination and route number on the front and main stages on the side. To stop the bus, you must signal to the driver. Get in at the front and put your ticket or tickets through the punching machine. When you want to get off, press the button on a column to alert the driver and alight from the middle or rear.

Taxis Finding taxis in Paris is quite a problem: they seem to vanish from the streets just when you most need them, in other words at lunchtime and in the early evening. The drivers work to suit themselves rather than the public; hence they avoid the rush hours, when traffic moves too slowly to clock up a profitable sum on the meter. As they belong to one of the most powerful closed shops in France, they can get away with this uncooperative behaviour.

The pick-up charge in Paris is currently 8f and the price per kilometre over 2f. A different rate, known as *tarif banlieu*, applies from the city to the suburbs and vice versa.

Airports and stations There are two international airports — Roissy-Charles de Gaulle 25 km (15 miles) to the northeast, and Orly 14 km (8 miles) to the south. You can reach the centre of Paris from both by RER; this conveniently links the airports with two of the mainline stations as well — Charles de Gaulle with the Gare du Nord and Orly with the Gare d'Austerlitz. There is also a bus service between

Charles de Gaulle and the Gare du Nord and Gare de l'Est stations, which takes about an hour.

Air France coaches run from Orly to Les Invalides air terminal (taking at least 40 minutes) and from Charles de Gaulle to Porte Maillot air terminal (at least 30 minutes). They ply direct between the two airports, which takes at least 50 minutes, although you should allow more time during rush hours and at weekends.

There are six major SNCF stations in Paris. These are the Gare du Nord for northern France, with connections to the UK and northern Europe; the Gare de l'Est for eastern France, Germany and beyond; the Gare de Lyon for south and southeastern France, Switzerland and Italy; the Gare d'Austerlitz for central and southwestern France and Spain; and the Gare de Montparnasse and St-Lazare for Brittany and Normandy.

All the mainline stations are on the Métro and/or RER. You should allow at least an hour to get from one station to another, apart from the Nord and Est stations which are within walking distance of each other.

For driving round Paris and parking in it, see pp. 56 and 57.

Bicycles

Cycling involves the emotions, if not the legs, of most French people. In July, the Tour de France is avidly followed throughout the country in the hope that it will be won, yet again, by a Frenchman (see p. 146). Cycling events on a smaller scale feature at countless village fêtes.

La bicyclette or *le vélo*, the bicycle, is a serious means of transport too. In fact, France is ideal terrain for the visiting cyclist — which is not to deny that it contains some testing hills. But the roads are quiet and scenic if you choose the minor ones, or furnished with cycle lanes if you have to ride on main ones; motorists are considerate; cycle shops, for hiring and repairs, are fairly plentiful; and, such is the reverence for two wheels, you will be assured of a warm reception at camp-sites, hotels and elsewhere.

Taking your own bike

Dedicated cyclists will want to take their own bicycles, ideally good touring models with drop handlebars and at least five gears. If yours is a new acquisition, keep the receipt to present at customs.

From the UK, the cross-Channel ferries usually carry bicycles free. Within France, you can avoid the boring bits by putting your bike on the train. It must be registered as ordinary baggage at the station, preferably several days before you depart, and will be sent through to your destination, usually arriving by a different train and after you do. SNCF guarantee to deliver it within 5 days if a connection has to be made, or within 24 hours (48 hours at peak periods) on a direct train. In certain cases — you have to inquire — you can travel on the same train as your bike: it then has to be registered only an hour before you leave. There is a charge for carriage by rail, except on a few local trains, where bikes are allowed to go free as hand luggage.

Equip yourself with spares, particularly a puncture kit. Bicycle repair shops are difficult to find in rural areas; in any case, they can't be relied on to stock British sizes of inner tubes and so on.

Insurance for your machine and yourself is important. The Cyclists' Touring Club supplies various travel policies. It also publishes an invaluable fact sheet on cycling in France and can suggest routes and contacts. Membership, for a modest fee, is open to UK and foreign residents. The CTC runs cycling holidays too, as do other organizations.

Renting a bike You can hire a bicycle at over 200 SNCF stations. You need to show proof of identity like a passport and leave a deposit; credit cards may be accepted. Children under 16 should have written authority from their parents as well. The rate is calculated per half day or day, payable on return of the machine.

It is sometimes possible to reserve a bike in advance, by writing direct to the station. And you might be allowed to start from one station and end up at another. The bicycles themselves are of basic unisex design (without a cross-bar), with adjustable handlebars and saddle; they are fitted with lights, lock and a luggage rack, but not necessarily gears. Touring models with ten-speed gears are sometimes available.

In most towns, bicycles can also be hired from a shop, which might have a better selection. Look for the sign *location de vélos*.

Cycling in France The rules of the road for cyclists are much as one would expect in any other country. British riders should remember to keep to the right!

However, you should not cycle in bus and taxi lanes, nor on foot-paths. You *must* use the cycle lane, where provided: this is marked by the sign *piste cyclable* (*obligatoire*). Normally, there will be no objection to your riding along canal towpaths.

Some special Franch hazards are the cobbled road surfaces in northern France, tramlines in many towns and level crossings. Paris is not recommended for the cyclist. In mountainous regions — and there are quite a few — you might encounter snow-blocked roads; check in advance for these on a Michelin map.

The best maps for cycling are the Michelin yellow maps (see p. 58). With them, you can pick the prettiest minor roads.

French motorists are not noted for courtesy to other road users. But the sight of a cyclist transforms them. They tend to give a honk on the horn when they come up behind, as a signal that they've noticed you: this is friendly, so don't take umbrage. They normally wait until there is plenty of room to spare before overtaking.

Many garages undertake cycle repairs. So does *un marchand de vélos* or bicycle shop.

Even a minimal amount of luggage can weigh down a bike. If you are aiming at a not-too-strenuous holiday, it's better to find a base where you can leave the bulky stuff and make excursions from there. Make sure you carry some thirst-quenching drink.

Clothing is a matter of common sense. But don't forget that it can be surprisingly chilly high up in the Pyrenees or the Alps, and that the sun can be unpleasantly strong in south and central France. Sunburn hits you in strange places, like the tops of the feet: you will need socks, sleeves, covering for the legs and a hat for protection. And sun-tan oil for the nose. There's no point in competing with French cyclists, who tend to be dressed to the nines in expensive sports gear.

Motorcycles and mopeds

Half the French population, at least, seem to own *un cyclomoteur*, a motorized bicycle which sounds like an angry lawnmower. This is the favourite vehicle of schoolchildren, since it can be ridden from the age of 14 without a licence, and of elderly peasants with long loaves strapped on their backs. In Paris these machines are a positive menace and on narrow country roads can get in your way quite effectively.

Le *vélomoteur*, 50–125 cc, is the next stage up, and *une moto*, short for *motocyclette*, is a 'real' motorbike. For these, there is an age limit and licences are required. They are much less common.

Motorbikes and mopeds of various types can be hired in many places from garages and specialist shops. Inquire at the tourist office. It is also very cheap, sometimes free, to transport your own by ferry across the Channel. In France, small machines, less than 50 cc, can be put in the luggage van of a train like a bicycle, and larger ones may go on the Motorail service.

Rules and regulations

Except for mopeds up to 50 cc, built not to exceed 45 km/h, a licence is necessary. A British one is acceptable. The minimum age is 18 for machines of 81 cc and over, and 16 for those of 51–80 cc.

Crash helmets of the approved kind, with reflecting headbands, are compulsory for driver and passenger.

If you are bringing your own motorbike, it must have third party insurance, and any passengers should be covered by insurance too. Motorcycles over 51 cc are treated in the same way as cars and must carry registrations plates and a foreign sticker.

The rules of the road are basically the same as for other vehicles in France (see p. 44). However, you should keep your headlights on, dipped, all the time. Light motorbikes, 51–80 cc, are restricted to a maximum speed of 75 km/h. Those under 50 cc are prohibited on motorways and must use cycle lanes where these exist.

At the filling station, two stroke is *le mélange deux-temps*.

Car rental

With big international firms like Avis, Hertz and Godfrey Davis Europcar well represented in France, car rental presents no difficulty. For air travellers, the major airlines do fly–drive packages, while SNCF offer its Train + Auto at main stations. All of these are bookable in advance. Holiday firms and travel agents can also arrange car hire.

Otherwise, there are many rental agencies within France, recognizable by the sign *location de voitures*. These may be cheaper than hiring from abroad, but possibly less reliable. The local tourist office will supply addresses.

The snag to hiring on the spot is that you have to pay a substantial deposit, in cash unless credit cards are accepted. Remember that prices are quoted *TVA en sus*, exclusive of value added tax (currently calculated at 18.6 per cent). Insurance cover is often fairly basic and you may be advised to take out extra insurance, which is costly. The rental company should provide any other necessary documents.

The minimum age at which you can rent a car is 21, although some firms impose their own limit of 23 or 25 and an upper one of 60 or 65. A full, not provisional, driving licence is obligatory (see p. 42) and you should take your passport as proof of identity.

There are often advantageous rates for unlimited mileage. It is usually possible, too, to collect the car in one place and leave it in another.

Renault have a popular scheme which allows you, in effect, to borrow a brand new car for an agreed sum and return it to the factory by a certain date. Contact their head office in your country for details.

Hitchhiking

Hitchhiking or *l'auto-stop* is legal in France, except on motorways, but is less easy than in some other countries. French car drivers are not known for their willingness to give lifts, partly because of their insurance requirements.

Lorry drivers are probably a safer bet. Fellow foreigners, whether tourists or truckers, might be more inclined to stop if you make your nationality obvious with a flag.

Provoya, a private concern based in Paris and with several regional offices, can arrange lifts by putting potential passengers in touch with drivers. There is a small fee.

Walking

Pedestrians

Pedestrians get a raw deal in France. There are two main types of road crossing, and plenty of them, but neither feel very safe.

Most pedestrian crossings or *passages à piétons* are incorporated with traffic lights. Here the danger is that cars can swoop round from either side on the same green light as the one that permits you to proceed on foot. Uncontrolled crossings are marked by studs or white stripes on the road, but you should never assert your right of way by stepping out on one in front of the traffic. If you happen to be run over on a crossing rather than the open road, you stand a better chance of winning your case against the driver — that's all.

Ramblers and hikers   For the long-distance walker, France is a land of opportunity. Some of its wildest beauty spots have been turned into national or regional parks, notably in the Pyrenees, Alps, Jura, Cévennes and Corsica. These are dedicated to the protection of historic sites and the traditional way of life and to the conservation of flora and fauna. Paths are clearly signposted and well maintained, with mountain refuges and information centres.

But walking is equally possible and pleasurable in many other parts of France, whose countryside is still remarkably unspoilt, if rather too full ot 'keep out' notices, particularly *chasse gardée*, reserved for hunting. The Michelin yellow maps are sprinkled with suitable *routes forestières* and *sentiers de grande randonnée* (forest walks and long-distance paths). Other paths (*petites randonnées*) have also been established by enthusiasts in many areas; details can be obtained from the local tourist office.

The French rambling association is the Comité National de Sentiers de Grande Randonnée. It publishes *topos-guides* to long-distance footpaths. The IGN (Institut National Géographique) has a series of useful maps — *cartes touristiques* and *topographiques*, maps covering forests, mountains, national and regional parks, and maps specifically for the enthusiastic walker. Recently a positive rash of books on the subject has appeared.

Various companies offer inclusive walking holidays and tours in France.

Staying Put – from Hotels to Tents

The essence of a French hotel is its individuality: no two are quite alike (though one might suspect that the same plumber had been at work). This diversity is a source of employment for numerous writers of guidebooks, endlessly describing their own favourites and discovering new ones. The risk of such personal assessments is that your fellow guest is your fellow reader, and the inn recommended as tranquil and unspoilt turns out to be heaving with tourists.

However, there are many other, less personal, guides to help in the search for somewhere to stay. Most useful is the trusty Michelin red guide (see also p. 59), which appears every spring. More idiosyncratic is the Gault-Millau *Guide France*, now published in English. Lists of officially approved hotels are available from the French Government Tourist Office, as well as the annual guide of the Logis et Auberges de France.

The latter is a national federation with nearly 5,000 members. It is typical of that pleasing French preference for a loose association of similar establishments, usually in private hands, rather than a chain of identical clones. The Logis are small-to-medium-sized tourist hotels, family-owned and mostly graded one- or two-star (see below). Tucked away in the provinces (there are none in Paris), they offer comfortable accommodation, which must meet certain standards, and good simple cooking, with the accent on regional dishes. The Auberges are smaller and plainer, but operate on the same principle of making guests feel at home.

The Relais Routiers, even more down-to-earth, also put out a guide every year. These are really transport cafés which cater, often excellently, for the hearty appetites of lorry drivers and sometimes provide basic accommodation. They are generally on main roads, so not the place for a quiet night.

Other groupings of distinctive character, higher up the scale, include Relais et Châteaux, castles and manors

Hotels

Choosing a hotel

in beautiful locations whose rates are remarkably competitive; Inter-Hotels, expensive but superbly run; France Accueil, two- and three-star, who, as part of the service, will book you into another hotel in the group at your next destination; Mapotel, all individually managed; and Les Petits Nids de France, over a hundred from one- to three-star.

Arcade, Campanile and Ibis are useful two-star groups, but anonymous. Novotel, Sofitel, Frantel and Mercure are more suitable for businessmen. Many of them have conference facilities and are situated in town centres or near motorways. Some visitors may be relieved to find outposts of the big internationals in France, like Hilton, Holiday Inn (expensive), Inter-continental and Trust House Forte, mainly in Paris and on the Riviera.

All hotels are classified by the French ministry of tourism into five grades. These go from one-star, fairly spartan but adequate, to four-star luxury at the height of grandeur. The star rating is shown on a plaque outside the door. Thus, for a two-star hotel, the requirements are a washbasin in all rooms, plus a bidet in 40 per cent of them; private shower or bath in 30 per cent of the rooms, of which 20 per cent should have their own toilet as well; at least one bathroom per 20 guests in rooms without facilities; at least one toilet per 10 rooms, with a minimum of one on each floor.

The prices of rooms are also officially controlled, except in four-star establishments. The tariff should be displayed at the hotel entrance or in the lobby and in the room itself.

The star classification is not given in the Gault-Millau and Michelin guides (and incidentally has nothing to do with Michelin's own system of stars), but it is used in other publications like the *Guide des Hôtels Logis et Auberges de France.*

Reservations   Advance booking is advisable for any part of France on the tourist track and essential during the holiday season, June to September, and at Easter. It is always necessary to make reservations for staying in Paris.

The long winter months can be difficult, too, when many hotels close down completely. Check opening times in the Michelin guide; it also tells you whether a place is shut on Sunday evenings or Mondays or another day of the week. Remember that the best hotels within a hundred miles of the capital are liable to be invaded by Parisians for the weekend.

Most of the hotels already mentioned have central booking offices, either in France or abroad, although not all accept reservations from the public. Otherwise, if you are writing direct to a hotel to book a room, it is best to do so in French (see p. 171). Enclose *un coupon-réponse international*, an international reply coupon, obtainable from post offices, and inquire about *le tarif des chambres*, the terms.

Assuming that the hotelier replies with confirmation of the booking, he will probably request *des arrhes*, a deposit, for a stay of any length. This should be the cost of approximately three nights room and breakfast or 4 nights full board. Send a banker's draft or a cheque written out in francs.

Telephone reservations are not legally binding. It's wise, even if you have a written booking, to reach the hotel by early evening, or else warn the management that you will be late.

Depending on your companions and circumstances, it can be more fun to look for a hotel on the spot. Arm yourself with the Michelin guide or consult the local tourist office and, if you possibly can, begin the search no later than four in the afternoon. Should you book by telephoning ahead, it's still sensible to arrive at the hotel by 6 p.m.; you can then inspect and if necessary reject the room, instead of registering.

Finding a hotel

Hotels are not always called *hôtels*. Indeed, *un hôtel* is also a private town mansion and a large public building, in particular the *hôtel de ville* or town hall. *Un motel* is, of course, a motel, although there are not very many in France. More common is *hôtellerie* or *hostellerie*, which used to mean a straightforward country inn and has now been coyly revived to denote a well-appointed hotel in rural surroundings (the sort beloved of weekending Parisians). *Une auberge* may carry a similar threat of rustic pretentiousness, although it can also be a simple place for board and lodging. *Un relais*, literally a staging post, has connotations of the coaching inn.

Une pension may range from a guest house to a proper hotel, but it generally belongs to a family and, by definition, provides meals. Not all hotels do, especially when they are simply known as *un hôtel*, and not *un hôtel-restaurant*; absence of a dining room is frequent in Paris and other cities. Ordinary hotels rarely have public rooms like a lounge either. Many restaurants, on the other hand, offer limited accommodation; this can be rudimentary despite a gastronomic accolade.

Bed and breakfast on the British model is not widely available. But you may see signs for *chambres d'hôte* or guest rooms, the nearest equivalent.

Arriving at the hotel

You should always ask to see the room before committing yourself, even if you've booked. Otherwise you will be taken for a fool and possibly put in the worst or most expensive room in the hotel. You should also inquire about the price and about any special rates — for families or children, or for longer stays. For three nights or over, *pension* terms are more economical but often restrict your choice of menu. You can have *pension complète*, full board, or *demi-pension*, half board. Find out as well whether breakfast is included in the price and whether dinner must be eaten in (you can also look this up in the Michelin guide).

To check in, you will have to leave an identity document at the reception desk, normally a passport. Alternatively, you will be asked to fill in *une fiche policière*, a hotel registration form (useful for tracking down criminals and the Jackal).

'I hope the plumbing's all right.'

Reproduced by courtesy of *Punch*

Then make sure you have parked your car in the proper place: what looks like a suitable spot on arrival could turn out to be illegal or in the middle of a market the next morning. If you intend going out for the evening, ask what the arrangements are for getting back into the hotel. Hotel staff often bolt the front door and go to bed about 10, or closet themselves with the television, which makes them oblivious to a frantic ringing of the bell when you're locked out.

Hotel bedrooms

You might require *une chambre à deux lits*, a double room; *une chambre avec un grand lit*, a room with double bed; or *une chambre simple/à un lit*, a single (not simple) room; or *deux chambres*, two rooms, with the same permutations. In practice, you often end up with a room containing one large bed, not quite big enough to qualify as a double, plus one or even two single beds.

You have to specify when you want a double bed, which can be embarrassing. But if, after doing so, you are allocated the typical French hotel room outlined above, you may be able to pay less by proving that you both slept in the same bed.

The French habit of cramming as many as possible into one hotel bedroom is fine for families or groups of friends; and, from the management's point of view, it means more paying heads in the dining room. However, the lone traveller will find accommodation more awkward. Many hotels simply don't have single rooms and can be reluctant to give away a double room to one person. Such single rooms as do exist may be little better than cardboard boxes, hastily and obviously carved out of a larger room.

Sheets (*les draps*) and blankets (*les couvertures*) tend to be ordinary enough, and a towel (*une serviette*), is usually supplied. The cupboard may yield an extra blanket and a pillow (*un oreiller*), which is still considered a soft option to the formidable French bolster. This is a hard cylinder of feathers which is as wide as the bed; not only is it uncomfortable, but you have to haggle with your partner over its position. If soap is not provided, you could ask for *une savonette*. Experienced guests carry their own light bulbs (both bayonet and screw type), as these can be very dim.

Noise can be a problem. Avoiding main roads and

railways, your search may bring you to the centre of a peaceful little town, where hotels are often found. Early the next morning, the square will start bustling and may be transformed into a market place. Motorbikes like to rev up under your window, and clocks will have chimed throughout the night to remind you of every passing quarter of an hour. If you demand a room at the back, *sur le derrière*, it's bound to be within earshot of the kitchens and overwhelmed by the smell of frying.

Plumbing Not so long ago, the message *tous conforts modernes* (every modern comfort) indicated that a hotel had hot and cold running, at least. Things have changed, and it is now normal to be offered a room *avec salle de bains*, with bathroom, *avec douche*, with shower, or *avec cabinet de toilette*, with basin and bidet. None of these, however, necessarily includes a toilet. This is usually stipulated, *avec WC*.

The bathtub or *la baignoire* is rare and tends to be the energetic hip-bath type, where you have to sit up and wash instead of stretching out for a soak. Much more common in French bedrooms is the *bidet*, both in hotels and in the home. If it's your first encounter with this fixture, be warned: it is designed for intimate ablutions and should not be mistaken for a toilet.

Showers are common, but prone to demonstrate the quirkiness of French plumbing by suddenly running hot or cold — or worse, belching out filthy water. Hotel toilets can be scarce, unhygienic and public in several respects, sometimes housed in a box in the middle of the landing; so it's a good idea to get a room with a private one.

Meals Any hotel that has a dining room, and particularly in the country, expects you to take your evening meal there. In the high season, failure to agree to this could lead to refusal of a room. Check in the Michelin guide, as you might want to explore the local restaurants.

Breakfast is nearly always available, even at those hotels without restaurants, and is occasionally quoted as part of the price of the room. It used to be customary to have it in your bedroom, but these days you're just as likely to share it with the vacuum cleaner in a deserted bar. Ask when you check in.

The average hotel breakfast or *le petit déjeuner*

comprises a choice of coffee, hot chocolate or tea, bread, rolls or *croissants*, butter and jam. It will probably be laid out on a red check tablecloth, without plates, and with bowls rather than cups for drinking from. It is permissible to dunk your crusts and retrieve the bits with a spoon. The butter will be delicious, despite being prewrapped in pats; the jam will inevitably be apricot, in individual pre-packed portions.

Marmalade is most unlikely, so too is anything more substantial. However, if you're staying in grander premises and money is no object, you could try asking for *confiture d'orange* (not *marmelade*, which is puréed fruit) and ordering *un oeuf à la coque*, a boiled egg, *un oeuf sur le plat*, a sort of fried egg, or *une tranche de jambon blanc*, a slice of ham.

Since a hotel breakfast is usually optional and relatively expensive, many people go to the nearest café. Here you can be sure of good coffee, either *un café au lait*, a large coffee with hot milk, or simply *un café*, a small black coffee, which might be *un express* made in an espresso machine. There is often a basket of *croissants* on the counter, although no one seems to mind if you bring in your own provisions fresh from the bakery. This enables you to sample *une brioche* or *un pain au chocolat* (see p. 124) with your breakfast.

Hoteliers, by the way, are usually quite amenable to the whims of travellers. They don't mind storing an ice-pack in the fridge for your cool box, and, if asked, will usually fill a thermos flask with coffee before your journey, or at least provide hot water.

Paying the bill

Hotel prices in France are very reasonable, and will certainly seem so to most visitors. A couple can be comfortably accommodated for 150f a night, or 200f for a room of minimum American standards. Obviously, rates go up in the high season and Paris always costs more.

The tariff shows the price per room, exclusive of meals, and may or may not include service charge and tax. The letters *TTC, toutes taxes comprises*, and *STC, service et taxe comprise* (service and tax included), explain the position. But when you come to settle the bill or *régler la note*, everything — service, tax, meals — will be added in.

For an overnight stay, the terms will be *chambre* (room), or *chambre et petit déjeuner* (room and breakfast) if applicable, plus *dîner* if you had an evening meal. You don't need to tip anyone, unless it is for a specific service like the porter carrying down the baggage. You can usually pay by credit card. Don't forget to ask for *le reçu*, the receipt.

Hostels There are something like 200 youth hostels or *auberges de jeunesse* in France, classified into three grades of comfort. Sleeping and cooking facilities vary, but none of them provide food. You should take your own sleeping bag, although bedding can often be hired.

In the high season, it is advisable to book in advance, by writing direct to the hostel concerned. The length of your stay is not limited, except in Paris where you might be restricted to a week.

Youth hostels are open to all members of the YHA and affiliated organizations such as the YMCA and YWCA. You must show your card and passport on arrival. You don't necessarily have to be youthful, at least only in spirit. However, people travelling by car are not admitted. Lists of hostels and further details can be obtained from the Youth Hostels Association.

Gîtes d'étape are hostels offering simple accommodation for ramblers, cyclists and travellers generally, anyone looking for a cheap overnight stop. The Fédération Nationale des Gîtes Ruraux publishes a booklet called 'Accueil à la Campagne', which lists *gîtes d'étape*, together with bed and breakfast places and farm camp-sites.

Self-catering Self-catering is big business in France: you can rent anything from a rustic shack to a modern apartment or luxury villa.

If you're looking for a holiday home, the quest could begin at the French Government Tourist Office, which keeps a full list of self-catering companies. These offer accommodation of all kinds throughout France, bookable in advance and usually as a package inclusive of travel.

One of the largest organizations is the semi-official Gîtes de France, with over 20,000 *gîtes* or homes on their books. These are privately owned cottages or flats, mostly in the rural depths or tiny villages and all with a minimum of running water, shower and inside toilet. They are inspected and graded by the federation. Annual membership gives access to the booking service which includes a reduction on ferry crossings when booking.

There is an English brochure detailing more than 1,800 properties reserved for the British section. Average weekly rent is £60—£100 per week.

If you dislike the idea of being 'packaged', you can write direct to one of the regional tourist committees in France for a list of accommodation in the area. The FGTO will supply addresses of these committees. The classified ads in newspapers are also a good source of information.

You can even take pot luck and find somewhere to rent on the spot, except in July and August when you would probably be unsuccessful. But with so many second homes, France has a lot of furnished accommodation available.

Look for the sign *à louer*, to rent, preceded by the description of the property — *appartement, studio, chalet, villa, maison* — which should be self-evident.

Popular winter and summer resorts are a good bet. Less obvious holiday areas also have potential. Several towns and villages run *gîtes communaux*, property belonging to the commune (it doesn't mean they are communal). The *mairie* (see p. 37) is an excellent place to begin. You could try an estate agent, *agent immobilier*, read the small ads in the local newspaper, or just ask around in cafés and shops. Consult the offical list of *gîtes ruraux* as well.

What to expect

The typical *gîte*, which is what many people plump for, will look like this: a modern stone-built cottage in traditional style, with shutters on the windows; bare stone walls, bare boards or tiles on the floors and no curtains; a big living-room-cum-kitchen, with an open fire and a large dining-table covered by an oiled cloth; beds in several rooms including the living room and maybe a sort of dormitory rather than separate bedrooms upstairs; a bathroom and toilet tacked on or squeezed in somewhere.

The absence of frills reduces housework to a minimum. The shutters not only provide security, but keep extremes of temperature and insects at bay. Sound-proofing is noticeably non-existent. There might be a patch of garden too, with a lawn or terrace and pots of geraniums; investigation usually reveals some interesting plants and herbs. But the first task on arrival is to get to grips with the various domestic systems.

Electricity   You will need to locate the mains switch to turn on the electricity. This is often up for ON and may automatically go off when there is a thunderstorm. So, if you find the house plunged into darkness, check the mains switch: it could be simply a matter of turning it on again to restore light. Make sure you know where the fuse box (*la boîte à fusibles*) is, in case of a blown fuse.

Electrical current is now 220—230 volts almost everywhere, as in the UK; in a few remote areas, it might still be 110 volts, the same as the US. Wiring colour codes are like those in Britain: brown is live and blue is neutral.

Plugs are the round 2-pin type (without an earth-wire), so you should take an adaptor along with your electrical gadgets. You can buy adaptors which convert to almost any voltage and type of socket — and they are cheaper in your home town than at the airport. Light bulbs or *ampoules électriques* are either the screw-in or bayonet kind.

Plumbing   Most French houses are plumbed directly to the mains and there is no cold-water storage tank. This means that a shower will suddenly run cold if someone else turns a hot tap on and reduces the pressure. It is advisable not to make too many demands on the system at once.

As in hotels, showers and bidets are more common than baths. *Les robinets*, taps, may require a little investigation before you find out how your particular ones work.

Trouble with the toilet is predictable and its cause, invariably, is the septic tank or *la fosse septique*. The answer is to flush nothing untoward down the toilet. Be careful, as well, to use the sort of cleaner specified by the owner or agent. If there is a second toilet, it might be the chemical kind which you have to empty yourself.

It's a good idea to find out where the stopcock or *le robinet d'arrêt* is.

The water might be heated by *le chauffe-eau*, water heater, either gas or electric immersion. *Une chaudière*, central-heating boiler, could be fairly primitive. Read the instructions carefully.

The kitchen   The cooker, generally run off bottled gas, will look rudimentary. There may be a lid covering the rings, which lifts up to form a splash-back. The grill, if it exists, will be inside the oven. This last tends to have three heat settings — off, on and very hot. Knobs are labelled O for *ouvert*, on, and F for *fermé*, off.

An electric kettle or toaster is an unlikely luxury. However, it's possible to make toast on an asbestos mat over a ring, which is a more suitable method for French bread anyhow. The open fire in the living-room could be the place for grilling fresh sardines and steaks. Or you might discover a barbecue outside, where you can burn *charbon de bois*, charcoal, obtainable from hardware stores (*drogueries*). For local flavour in the south, try grilling over *sarments de vigne*, vine shoots, obtained from a friendly winegrower.

The kitchen will be well equipped with pots and pans, sharp knives, a chopping board, coffee pot, salad spinner, cork screw and so on, all indicative of French priorities in cooking. Some gadgets may be unfamiliar, like the *mouli légumes*, designed to purée vegetables for soup. The French tin opener is a neat little instrument and very effective when mastered; but you may prefer to bring your own.

Le frigo, fridge, will be conventional, though small by American standards and without much in the way of a freezing compartment. If there is one, *la machine à laver*, washing machine, could be rather antiquated, operating on the principle of boiling and pounding; so be careful about putting in delicate or brightly coloured garments.

The store cupboard will probably contain a few essentials such as salt and pepper, dried herbs, oil, mouldy jam and anything else left behind by the previous occupants. But, if you and your family depend on items like tea, tomato ketchup, marmalade, peanut butter, cornflakes, baked beans, you must bring your own supplies, since these are difficult or expensive to buy in France.

The disposal of rubbish or garbage, fittingly known as *les ordures*, can be a problem. At many *gîtes* you'll find a compost heap, for vegetable waste, and a bonfire site, for burning paper. Very rarely is there a refuse collection or *un ramassage des ordeurs*, except in towns; if there is, it may be an inadequate once a fortnight. However, it's worth inquiring of the owner/agent or in the neighbourhood.   *Garbage*

You'll probably have to make several trips to the public garbage dump. This is normally situated in a beauty spot and is easily scented out despite the lack of signposting. With luck, there might be a large metal rubbish container in the nearest village, which you can visit instead.

Locks and keys

You might encounter difficulties with the front door key or *la clef*. French keys often turn anti-clockwise to lock. The same applies to door handles.

Emergencies

People like the plumber, electrician and gas man (*le plombier, l'électricien, l'employé de gaz*) often live locally. Consult the owner or agent of the property or a neighbour, or look up the yellow pages of the phone directory. Workmen are usually sympathetic, but remember they might be less so if called out on a Monday or during the lunch break.

Camping and caravanning

Camping makes the unthinkable affordable — exotic or, at any rate, foreign locations, mobility (but with the familiarity of your own car), and happy children too. This is its attraction for the thousands of British families who take a tent or caravan across the Channel every year.

Camping (*le camping*) is very popular among the French themselves, although usually in a version far removed from communion with nature. Their caravans are like second homes, kitted out with all the paraphernalia from television to toilets (one wonders why they have to occupy camp-sites at all); and they seem to spend their time preparing full-scale meals, which are consumed at proper tables and chairs under everyone's gaze.

For this reason, it's important to reserve your pitch in advance during July and August. The notorious congestion of the Riviera is not representative of the whole of France, but there's no doubt that some sites get very crowded. You should write direct to the site, enclosing an international reply coupon (see p. 79). Some owners insist on advance bookings, although a few will not accept them, notably at the Bois de Boulogne in Paris.

The alternative is to book an inclusive camping holiday or, particularly if you're not motorized, to rent equipment on the spot (see p. 16). Otherwise, of course, you can take a chance on finding somewhere when you arrive.

Two indispensable handbooks are the Michelin *Camping Caravanning France*, an annual selection, and the comprehensive *Official French Camping and Caravanning Guide*. Both are in French only, but easily understood.

Choosing a site

Castels et Camping Caravaning is a group consisting of over 40 high-quality sites, set in the grounds of châteaux and historic houses. The Touring Club de France (TCF) runs a similar number of luxury sites, including one in the capital at the Bois de Boulogne. Another association is the Fédération Nationale de l'Hôtellerie de Plein Air (FNHPA); as well as some first-class sites, they provide static caravans and chalets for rent.

Those interested in camping on a farm will find details in the official French guide mentioned above. Further information is obtainable from Agriculture et Tourisme and from the Fédération Nationale des Gîtes Rureaux. The Fédération Française de Naturisme caters for nudists.

Most of these organizations publish lists of their sites. The French Government Tourist Office has a useful fact sheet on camping and caravanning.

Official campsites are classified from one- to four-star. As a basic minimum, you can expect covered washing and toilet facilities and a daily refuse collection. Four-star sites offer full amenities, among them hot showers, telephones, a shop and playground, and possibly a bar or restaurant, launderette and swimming pool. This can cost more than a hotel. You should allow 55f a day for a one-star site, 95f for a four-star. All graded sites limit the density of campers per hectare, although this restriction becomes more elastic at peak periods. All are required by law to display their star rating and charges at the entrance.

Types of site

Aire Naturelle (AN) sites are official grounds, but with the emphasis on their natural surroundings. *Camping à la ferme* (camping on farm land) may or may not be recognized and in either case is likely to be very simple. However, a farmer will often grant you a field to yourself, and it is a nice compromise between the untamed wilderness and the security of a site. Do not disdain the *campings municipeles*, town campsites. These are usually cheap and may be pleasantly situated by a river; they are convenient as well, especially for forays to restaurants in town.

Off-site camping, called *le camping sauvage*, is scarcely mentioned in the guidebooks. Indeed, it is prohibited in many areas and would be foolhardy in the south of France. But in other parts, for example, the Ardèche and Brittany, it is allowed. Always seek permission from the owner before pitching a tent on private land. Otherwise, try the *mairie* and, in *forêt domaniale* or state forest, apply to the local Office des Eaux et Forêts.

If you fancy a winter trip in your caravan, suitable sites or *caravaneige* are listed in the official guide.

Finding a site
If you have not pre-planned, you will relish the freedom of last-minute discovery. It should not be too difficult, with nearly 9,000 graded sites and many others to choose from.

A good starting point is the local tourist office, which will be able to tell you about sites in the vicinity. Even without the camping handbooks, you can see whether a reasonable site exists by checking under the *lieux de séjour*, places to stay, in the Michelin green guide. On the road, you can hardly miss the ubiquitous *camping* sign and symbol.

The French ministry of tourism operates an information scheme in the summer, giving current availability of space on campsites throughout the country. There are centres on motorways and main roads, and you can also dial *allô camping* telephone numbers for different regions. The radio station France Inter, on 1829 metres longwave, broadcasts special bulletins after the news and mans a help-line which you can ring for camping and traffic reports. The service is described in the FGTO leaflet.

Prices
Most classified sites are now free to fix their own prices, and these vary considerably. But they must be posted up at the gate, so you can study them before deciding, rather as you would a menu outside a restaurant.

Charges generally run from midday to midday. They might be quoted separately, per person, plus the car, and tent or caravan, or there might be an inclusive rate per pitch. Sometimes the use of showers or electricity is extra. Children under seven normally get a reduction. You should inquire about special rates for a longer stay.

You will need to show proof of identity when you arrive and may even have to surrender your passport.

The camping *carnet* is, in effect, a passport to instant acceptability. Not only is it an identity document, but it also provides evidence that you are covered by third-party insurance. *The international camping carnet*

At some sites, including those belonging to Castels et Caravanning Camping, the carnet is compulsory. You may get a discount by producing it. It is valuable too for off-site camping and could be the crucial factor in winning you the necessary authorization.

The *carnet* is renewable each year and can be obtained through motoring, camping and caravanning organizations.

Butagaz and Camping Gaz are widely sold at hardware shops (*drogueries*), service stations and campsite shops. Camping Gaz, a French product, is also cheaper than it is in Britain. Shell Butane is sold, but you will have trouble finding the right size of screw-top cylinder. Paraffin (*pétrol* or *pétrollampant*) can be difficult to obtain. *Equipment*

Shops on site often stock basic essentials, toiletries, groceries and so on. Inevitably, they are more expensive than ordinary stores.

Hitch a caravan to your car and the customs procedure is the same as for a car on its own (see p. 42). No additional documents are required, although you must have adequate insurance for the caravan and trailer. If the caravan is a borrowed one, you should carry written permission from the registered owner. It's also a good idea to bring the caravan log book and inventory. *Taking a caravan*

The dimensions and weight of a caravan must not exceed certain limits. The towing vehicle should be fitted with an adequate rear-view mirror.

Special rules of the road for caravans in France are as follows. On motorways and main roads, you must keep a distance of 50 metres behind the vehicle in front. You are not allowed to drive in the outer left-hand lane of a motorway. Caravans are banned from Paris. Speed limits are the same as for cars, except in the case of very heavy caravans, i.e. those which exceed the weight of the towing vehicle by more than 30 per cent. These are restricted to a maximum of 45 km/h (28 mph), and must carry a speed limit sign to that effect on the back. It is not permitted to leave a caravan overnight in a lay-by. However, some towns allocate parking spaces for caravans. Many of the *aires de repos*, rest areas, on motorways are also suitable for a one-night stop.

A car with caravan falls into category 2 in terms of motorway tolls (see p. 54). A motor caravan counts as the slightly more expensive category 3.

The motoring organizations and their continental handbooks are a fund of useful advice for caravan owners.

Leaving a caravan in France

Temporary importation, as outlined above, ceases to apply after six months. If you want to leave your caravan on site in France for future visits, complications about VAT and insurance arise. Contact the French embassy for information.

Camper vans and minibuses

Recent legislation states that all vehicles constructed to carry ten or more people, driver included, must be fitted with a tachograph. This is the monitoring device that lorry drivers have resisted so strongly. Check with the consulate whether you are affected by the regulations.

UK law also requires that the driver of a vehicle adapted to carry nine or more passengers should hold a public service vehicle driving licence, in addition to a normal licence.

Eating

Ask a Frenchman to list his leisure activities and the chances are that he will mention food. Most French people, whatever their social background, are genuinely interested in eating.

They love talking about it, too. In France, unlike some other countries, it's not considered rude to discuss the finer points of a meal while consuming it; in fact, it's positively polite. If you say you're on a diet, everyone will be fascinated, probably swapping details of their own attempts to lose weight.

Their attitude to food is an odd mixture of reverence and routine acceptance. Paul Bocuse, the showman of the new-style cooking, is fêted like a film star and has been officially honoured by the state, like that other great chef, Escoffier, before him. Yet those other luminaries of the new cooking, the Troisgros brothers (one of whom died recently), run their establishment from the old station hotel in Roanne, an ugly industrial town north-west of Lyon. For the French, eating out is an everyday experience and, although Sunday lunch at a local restaurant may be the high point of the week, it's always a family affair with children and grannies and everybody. Home entertaining, on the other hand, is for formal occasions.

The lack of mystique about lunching or dining out makes life much easier for the foreigner. For a start, you can be sure of finding at least one reasonable eating-place in any town of modest size; it might even be excellent. Restaurants need not be expensive either. Fifty francs should buy you a proper five course meal with wine and, of course, it's possible to eat more cheaply with some research. Children are no problem. The French are dotty about babies, so the younger they are, the warmer the welcome they'll get.

The *nouvelle cuisine*, literally new cooking, hit the headlines in the 1970s and has since spread beyond France to influence many of the world's top restaurants.

The nouvelle cuisine

Basically, it is a manner of cooking characterized by lightness of touch and purity of style, a reaction against the cloying sauces and elaborate garnishes of classical *haute cuisine*; it demands the finest and freshest ingredients, cooked so as to enhance their natural flavours, sometimes very rapidly in the oriental way; and it requires meticulous care in preparation and in presentation, which is often in small portions.

The *nouvelle cuisine* should not be confused with *cuisine minceur*, the invention of Michel Guérard. Mainly by replacing high-calorie elements and methods with non-fattening ones, this bends the rules to prove that slimming is compatible with gourmet food.

However, Guérard also belongs to the clique of owner-chefs who are the leading exponents of the *nouvelle cuisine*. Led by Bocuse, it includes the Troisgros, Chapel, the Haeberlin brothers, Vergé, Girardet and Bise. They each have their own specialities. Bocuse is famous for sea bass stuffed with lobster mousse and wrapped in pastry, the Troisgros for salmon with sorrel and for *terrine* of vegetables, the Haeberlins for spit-roasted truffled chicken with noodles and *foie gras*. The new cooking can be just as rich as the old, if not as heavy.

The *nouvelle cuisine* even has its own bible, the annual *Guide-France* by the journalists Henri Gault and Christian Millau, who first dreamt up the phrase *nouvelle cuisine*. Under their system, restaurants are marked out of 20, from 10 at the bottom to 19 at the top. *Toques* or chef's hats are bestowed, red for *nouvelle cuisine*, white for *cuisine classique*, with four *toques* as the ultimate accolade.

The *nouvelle cuisine* has had a tremendous, if not always beneficial, impact. In the wrong hands, it borders on the ridiculous and many costly and pretentious menus are concocted in its name. As practised by the chosen few, it is a gourmet's paradise, if you enjoy and can afford that sort of thing. But, like any other trend, its real effect is much more limited than all the media hype would suggest. It is a branch of *haute cuisine*, confined to the highest levels of the restaurant trade, both in France and abroad.

Meanwhile, the vast majority of people prefer the conventional cookery which, at its best, is far more representative of what French food is all about. It might be described as an amalgam of *cuisine bourgeoise*, good

honest fare, and *cuisine régionale* (regional cookery),
with perhaps a dash of *cuisine paysanne* (peasant
cooking) and *cuisine improvisée* (improvization). Thus,
most restaurants continue to serve their *gigot d'agneau*
and *tarte aux pommes* (roast leg of lamb and apple tart)
and most housewives to cook their *coq au vin* (chicken
in wine) at home, regardless of fashion. The best-selling
cookbooks are not those of Bocuse and his fraternity
but classics like *La Vraie Cuisine de Tante Marie* (roughly,
'Aunt Mary's good cooking'). And the general movement
towards lighter, simpler food in France has more to do
with the pressures of modern living and awareness of
health than with a fashion among top chefs.

Cuisine régionale

French cookery is rooted in the provinces, and one of
the main reasons for this is the quality of local produce.
Distribution operates on an almost parochial scale, even
though Paris exerts its usual pull on the nation. Farmers'
cooperatives are widespread and individual peasants still
bring their bundles of leeks or baskets of eggs to market.
People tend to shop daily, despite the fact that most of
them now own fridges, so freshness is ensured.

Cuisine régionale is firmly established if only because
restaurants in France, wherever they may be, can count
on regular custom. However, you should not expect to
be regaled with *cassoulet* (a rich stew of haricot beans
and different meats) as soon as you hit Toulouse.
Specialities are not the staple diet, for many of them are
exactly that — reserved for special occasions. Others
have become tourist traps, like the exorbitantly|priced
foie gras (goose liver) on sale by every roadside in the
Dordogne. Some are really peasant fare, using up bits
and pieces; the *alycot* of Languedoc, for example, is a
stew of chicken gizzards, which you would be most
unlikely and unlucky to encounter. And the chances
are that wherever you go you may be offered *soupe de
jour* (soup of the day), usually vegetable, *côte de porc*
(pork chop), *crème caramel*, or any of the other standard
dishes that turn up with monotonous predictability all
over France.

Nevertheless, there is a distinctive feeling to the
cookery of each region. The best way to identify the
local flavour is to do some shopping yourself (see p. 122).
You can then see and try many of the ingredients that
will inform the restaurant menu.

Charcuterie
and cheeses

Every region specializes in some sort of *charcuterie* —
hams, sausages and other pork products too diverse to
describe. The most famous perhaps is *jambon de Bayonne*,
Bayonne ham, from the southwest corner of France.

Cheeses are equally characteristic of their place of
origin. The chalky Camembert and bland Saint-Paulin
from Normandy and the creamy Brie from the Ile-de-
France are marketed and copied throughout France and
abroad, and feature on nearly every cheeseboard. So too
do Roquefort, the expensive but exquisite blue sheep's-
milk cheese, the mild Reblochon from the Alps, and the
Norman Pont-l'Evêque, reminiscent of the cowshed. All
these are fairly commercialized, although you might
get *fermier* or farm interpretations near their source.

But any worthwhile restaurant will include local
cheeses in its selection, often the sort that don't travel.
Inevitably, there is a goat's-milk cheese or *chèvre*, especially if you are in central or western France where it is
called Chabichou or Cabécou. It may come in the shape
of a pyramid or a log and can be fresh and salty, or aged
and powerfully goaty. In the Alps, you would un-
doubtedly be presented with one of the smooth Tommes,
the holey Comté or the rich Vacharin; in the Auvergne,
it would be the veined Bleu d'Auvergne, the hard Cantal
or Salers; in the north, the taste is for strong cheeses like
Maroilles, Dauphin and Vieux Lille, to be washed down
with beer; in Alsace and Lorraine, they favour the spicy
Munster and Géromé.

Regional
specialities —
inland

The *charcuterie* and the cheeses are just two of the
glories of France. They illustrate the essentially rustic
nature of regional food, since both were originally
evolved as a means of preservation. More sophisticated
main-course dishes tend to be the product of prosperous
areas and many have gained a wider reputation, like
boeuf bourguignonne from Burgundy, appropriated by
the Parisians and shortened to *bourguignon*, but still a
beef stew in red wine. A recent revival in the Dordogne
is the *magret* or *maigret*, a sort of duck steak; but the
Périgord truffles are a prohibitive price, and anything
labelled *aux truffles* will doubtless contain only a tiny
sliver of that much vaunted fungus.

Freshwater fish are less in evidence that the guidebooks suggest, except for the obligatory trout. It would
be a rare treat to come across the Alpine version of the

salmon, known as *lavaret*. Similarly, the unusual game birds one reads about seem to have been trapped in print rather than reality. You are more likely to be offered *pintadeau*, guinea fowl, which is bred on a large scale. The mountain antelope or *chamois* is now rare and goat is a more profitable substitute. The 'wild' boar that you sometimes see hanging in game shops may have been farmed.

The coast is more dependable for specialities. One of the joys of arriving in France afer a Channel crossing is to tuck into a *plateau de fruits de mer* (seafood platter), a mountain of shellfish so diverse that it's hard to believe they come from the same Channel. Two less familiar ones are *palourdes* and *vernis*, both types of clam. *Moules*, mussels, and *huîtres*, oysters, seem to be always in season. The latter are graded by size on menus, from 00 (the largest) to 6 (the smallest), and often called after the place where they were cultivated, such as Belons and Armoricaines from Brittany and Marennes from near La Rochelle. *Seafood*

The pride of Brittany is its lobsters; hence the famous *homard à l'armoricaine*, corrupted to *à l'américaine* according to your point of view. Lobsters are quoted *SG* on menus, which means priced by weight or *selon grosseur*. And fish may be available on the menu *selon arrivage*, depending on the catch.

The Mediterranean is equally abundant in seafood, from the spiny *rascasse* and other nameless specimens fit only for the numerous fish soups of the south, to the excellent sea bass (*loup de mer*, also known as *bar* in the west), the red mullet (*rouget*) and the ugly John Dory (*Saint-Pierre*). Only the Italians have really suffered the effects of the polluted Med so far, but it's sensible to steer clear of raw shellfish, particularly mussels.

One fish which turns up on countless menus throughout France is *lotte*, which may be translated as monkfish or angler fish. A large creature with a grotesque mouth, its flesh is firm and white and free of bones. It has also become quite expensive, almost on a par with the scampi for which it sometimes stands in.

Meat is a more general commodity, less tied to a particular place, and some is even imported, much to French farmers' displeasure. Among Europeans the French are *Meat* second only to the Belgians in meat consumption, if not yet on a level with the Americans. On the whole, quality is high, as a visit to the butcher's will prove, although it might not appear so when you're confronted with an anonymous *bifteck* (steak) on your plate.

Nevertheless, you might notice the difference if it was a Charollais steak, which would probably be indicated on the menu. This breed, originating in Burgundy, is reputedly the finest for beef. Pauillac on the Gironde estuary, usually associated with the great red wines of Bordeaux, is known for salt-meadow lamb or *agneau de pré-salé*.

The French preference for undercooking their meat is particularly apparent with lamb. If you're ordering a steak or similar, ask for *bien cuit*, well done; *à point*, medium to rare; *saignant*, very rare; or *bleu*, practically raw. Venison, hare and other game, you might be relieved to know, is normally fresh and is not hung until high in the British manner.

One veal chop tastes much like the next. Veal is widely available in France, more so than in Britain at any rate, and the French don't feel the same qualms about cruelty to calves.

Sweet specialities

These abound. Every town seems to have its own variety of cake, biscuit, bread, pancake, tart, candy or sweetmeat. Some have travelled further, like the *nougat* of Montélimar, the *madeleines* of Commercy, immortalized by Proust, and the now common *tarte Tatin*, an upside-down apple tart, invented near Orléans. Brittany is the home of sweet and savoury pancakes, *crêpes* and *gallettes*; Lorraine has a reputation for jams and preserved fruits, the Agenais for prunes.

Appellation contrôlée

It is not often realized that the *appellation* system of quality control applies to food as well as to wines (see p. 111). *Appellation d'origine contrôlée*, to give its full title, but usually abbreviated to *AC* or *AOC*, confers a specific legal definition on a product and protection at national and international level; it stipulates the place of origin and regulates the variety or breed and the methods of manufacture or production.

Among foods with their own *appellation* are Bresse chickens, Charentes butter and walnuts from Grenoble. The biggest category covered by the *AC* system, outside wine, is cheese. To date 24 cheeses have been deemed worthy, including well-known ones like Brie, Roquefort and Pont-l'Evêque, and less well-known ones such as Chaource, Selles-sur-Cher, Beaufort and Saint-Nectaire.

It is impossible to do justice here to the wealth of regional cooking in France. If you want to know more, a great many books have been written to enlighten you on the subject. The Michelin green guides contain a helpful introduction to the specialities of each region.

Information

Cuisine à la française is that unfortunate creation which passes for French cooking in many restaurants outside France. It is easily confused with international *cuisine*, the stock-in-trade of hotels the world over, with their *avocat aux crevettes, steak Diane* and *crêpes Suzette*. So successfully have the French propagated the idea of their own supremacy in culinary matters that, for the past century at least, any establishment with pretensions would offer a 'French' menu.

Cuisine à la française and how to avoid it

Inside France, you also run the risk of being conned. The French have always been particularly disdainful about English food but, whatever your nationality, you may be taken for an obvious foreigner on whom unscrupulous restaurateurs will vent their prejudices. Paris and the big resorts are danger spots, and those expensive, pompous *menus gastronomiques* are often intended to capture innocents abroad. You should generally avoid these, as well as the *menus touristiques*. Main roads and city centres are not the place to find a reliable restaurant, whereas back streets, country towns, ports and station precincts are. Save up your francs, if you will, for a serious repast at one of the be-toqued and be-starred recommendations in the guidebooks. But don't ignore the single knife and fork and the red R for good value in the Michelin. They are often a better clue to authentic regional cooking, more basic perhaps, but just as rewarding.

The typical French restaurant, owned and run by a family, still flourishes in the provinces. How do you find it? Having consulted the guidebooks and explored the back streets, the best method is personal inspection. Every eating place, from the grandest to the humblest, must by law display a menu with prices outside. This

Finding a restaurant

you can study at your ease, even looking up unknown words in the dictionary, before deciding. A printed menu is a bad sign: it should be hand-written, preferably in purple ink. The shorter it is, the more likely that the food is personally prepared.

Don't be put off by the appearance and décor of a restaurant. French taste can be awful, so it is not significant. A better gauge of merit is how crowded the dining room is. It's useful to do some initial research in the eating guides, which will give you a notion of prices and tell you about closing dates. And don't be ashamed to brandish the Michelin or Gault-Millau inside: it proves you're serious.

There is no official grading of restaurants, as there is of hotels and campsites. However, various types of establishment can be distinguished.

Le restaurant   This, by definition, serves full meals at set times and has a proper menu. You can't go there just for a drink, nor for a single dish. It might call itself an *auberge* or *hostellerie*, especially in the country where it would probably be combined with a hotel. If it were olde-worlde and rustic, it could be a *taverne*, and near a motorway it would be a *restoroute*. *Routiers* or *relais routiers* are primarily for lorry drivers and have a good reputation, not always well founded.

The words *grill(-room)* or *rôtisserie* don't necessarily imply that the restaurant is confined to grills or roasts. However, *grillades au feu de bois* is charcoal grilling. The mention of *un cadre soigné*, a well-kept setting, hints at some degree of luxury. But *la terrasse* simply indicates tables and chairs outside, usually on the pavement in the case of a café.

Le café   *Le café* is a social institution: a place for drinking and eating and whiling away the time, where you can meet friends or take the family or linger alone and undisturbed — except for the juke box, *baby-foot* (bar football) or TV, recent installations to attract a waning trade. Children are quite acceptable, but those under 14 are not allowed alcohol, as the *avis aux mineurs* (advice to minors) notice warns. The *tarif des consommations*, listing prices for drinks, must be displayed by law.

As well as coffee, there is a vast array of drinks, from the intoxicating to the soft. You can prop up *le zinc*, the bar, which is cheaper, or sit down and be waited on. But you can't buy a drink at the bar and then sit down or, if you do, you'll be charged accordingly. If you're having more than one round, pay for them all together at the end, not after each one. The service charge is usually included and should be shown by *SC, service compris* or *prix nets* on the bill or price list. Food is basic, along the lines of *un sandwich*, half a French loaf filled invariably with a slice of ham, and *un croque-monsieur*, a toasted cheese and ham sandwich, plus ice creams.

Also a brewery, this has come to mean a large café-restaurant providing drinks, among them beer, coffee and light meals throughout the day. *Choucroute garnie*, sauerkraut with ham and sausage, is typical. *Un buffet*, at stations and airports, could be described as a smaller version of the *brasserie*. At the station too, and elsewhere, you will come across *une buvette*, a stall or kiosk with drinks and perhaps ice creams and sandwiches. *Un bistro(t)* is technically a small café-restaurant for wine and simple meals, although it could turn out to be a smart little joint in the city. *La brasserie*

Here you repair for a quick drink, sitting on a tall chair or standing at the counter. It may be merely a corner of the tobacconist's, and food or coffee is rare. *Un estaminet* is the northern equivalent of a tavern, with connotations of being a low dive. *Le bar*

By way of contrast, this is a prim tea room or coffee shop, normally part of a cake shop, where you can sit down to partake of expensive cakes and ices at any time of day. Afternoon tea, the meal, known as *le goûter*, plays no part in the daily routine. It is restricted to a few ladies, and to children, who will be silenced in mid-afternoon with bread and a slab of chocolate (a memorable combination). *Le salon de thé*

The French do not excel at snacks, being more concerned with higher things. However, *casse-croûte à toute heure* widely advertises the fact that snacks are available at any time of day. Pizzas are now common and so are French fries or *frites*; you can ask for *cinq/dix francs de frites* (5/10 francs worth). *Plats à emporter* means takeaway or take-out food, sometimes sophisticated dishes *Snacks and fast food* ready prepared for the hostess who wants to impress. *Crêperies*, for sweet and savoury pancakes, have extended beyond Brittany, their real home, to many tourist areas.

Modern intrusions on the eating scene are *la cafétéria* and *le snack* or *snack-bar*, both specializing in quick meals and drinks. The self-service café or *libre-service* tends to be found on the outskirts of a town or in a hyper-market. *Le drug-store* offers a mixture of American fast food — spare ribs, hot dogs, hamburgers — and straight-forward French dishes. The overall standard of such places is high (certainly by comparison with the UK) and you can get good food at reasonable prices.

Alternatives   You might, in the course of your travels, happen on a sign with the words *table d'hôte*, pointing down an intriguing farm track. Host's table, for that is the literal translation, was the old practice whereby several people ate a meal together at a fixed price. Today, it calls for boldness and some command of spoken French, for it is an opportunity to enjoy excellent home cooking and the company of the host and family. (*Hôte* means host, landlord, and guest, both male and female, in a hotel; when invited to a home, a guest is *un invité/une invitée* or, for a meal, *un(e) convive*.) A *table d'hôte* spirit sometimes prevails in country restaurants, where the *patron* himself will lavish the courses upon you and join in for the odd drink.

You will often see the message *dégustation* by the road, *de vins* in wine-growing regions, or *de huîtres, de fruits de mer*, on the coast, or some other local speciality. The term is used for tasting, sampling, with the idea of relishing the process. It could be the prelude to larger purchases, or just a quick refreshment stop.

How to eat   As soon as you walk into a restaurant, you will probably
French   be greeted by a waiter or waitress or, very often, by the owner in person. If you've booked a table, tell them *J'ai réservé une table*. Otherwise, simply ask for *Une table pour deux/quatre personnes, s'il vous plaît*, a table for two/four please, or however many it may be. You will then be ushered to a table. If nobody meets you at the door, it's better to hover around there and wait rather than march straight up to a vacant table.

Because eating is treated seriously in France, most restaurants have only one sitting. It's unlikely that you will be hurried through your meal in order to free the table for more customers, and if you are you should resist. So you might be told that the restaurant is full (*complet*) even when it appears relatively empty, the reason being that the other tables have already been reserved. There is then no alternative but to find another restaurant. Sometimes, however, you might be advised to wait, or have a drink in the bar if there is one.

Every restaurant must offer *un menu*, a set menu or fixed-price meal, as well as *une carte*, an à la carte menu. Nine times out of ten, you get better value and food by choosing the first rather than the second method. You can't mix the two, unless you have reached an agreement with the proprietor.

Le menu and la carte

   If you do opt for *la carte*, you will find that the main dish or *plat* comes *garni*, that is with vegetables. You might feel satisfied with this on its own and order nothing else. You are perfectly entitled to have just one course, but you might not be very popular, especially in a small restaurant which puts its effort and pride into the *menu* rather than the *carte*.

   In all but the simplest places providing a single *menu du jour* (set menu of the day), there will be two or three *menus* covering a range of prices, say 40, 60 and 80f. An extra course may be the only difference between them. They could be labelled *menu touristique* or *gastronomique* — treat both with caution — or *menu dégustation*, a run through the specialities of the house, in small helpings.

   The average *menu* consists of four courses, although it can rise to seven for a full feast. Don't let these numbers put you off: a good French meal is balanced and the portions are not large, particularly of the meat course. The salad seems to lighten the stomach and you need only have a nibble of the cheese. Enjoy the meal in a leisurely way, as the French do, and you won't feel bloated.

   Every meal includes bread.

   A full menu breaks down, in this order, as follows:

1 Hors d'oeuvre
Could be a tomato salad; *céleri rémoulade*, raw celeriac in mustardy mayonnaise; *crudités*, raw vegetables; *pâté maison* or *terrine*, usually home-

made; or melon. At lunch there may be a copious selection, from which you take several. At dinner this course may be replaced by soup.

2 Soup

Soupe is substantial; *potage* supposedly more refined and often homemade vegetable; *crème* is cream soup; and *consommé is clear*, served more often in the evening. *Soupe/potage du jour* is invariably a thick vegetable soup and the tureen may be brought round again for a second helping.

3 *Entrée*

A choice of fish, shellfish, snails, frogs' legs, eggs. In most restaurants these first three courses would all be grouped together in one category, perhaps under the heading *pour commencer*, to start; however, a more expensive *menu* would include two consecutive courses before the main dish.

4 Main course

Often in fact called *entrée*. Meat, poultry, ham or game, roast or grilled, or fish.

5 *Légumes*

Vegetables may be served separately but generally accompany the main dish. *Pommes frites* or *sautés* (French fries or sauté potatoes) are predictable, also *pommes vapeur*, plain boiled potatoes. The standard green vegetable, if there is one at all, is *petits pois*, peas, or *haricots verts*, French or greenbeans.

6 *Salade*

Almost always a distinct course consisting of a simple green salad, dressed with *vinaigrette*, oil and vinegar. Sometimes you can add your own dressing from bottles on the table. Mayonnaise, often homemade, is reserved for shellfish and other starters. Salad cream or thousand island dressing is unheard of and should not be requested (nor should ketchup).

7 *Fromage*

The cheeseboard is, or should be, the glory of a French restaurant (see p. 96). It may be left on the table for you to select and you can take more than one; don't be afraid to seek the waiter's advice. It is normal to eat cheese with a knife and fork, but you can ask for more bread, *encore du pain, s'il vous plaît*, if it's not forthcoming.

8 Dessert

Known as *entrements* in plusher places, or sometimes as *douceurs*. Common are *mousse au chocolat*, chocolate mousse; *crème caramel*; *négresse en chemise*, chocolate and cream or ice cream in some combination; *ananas au kirsch*, pineapple, could be tinned, with kirsch; *fruits rafraîchis*, fruit salad; *tarte aux pommes/aux fruits*, apple/fruit tart; and always *glaces*, ice creams, and *sorbets*, water ices. When you reach the sweet course, the waitress will probably inquire *Qu'est-ce que vous désirez/prenez comme dessert?* She will then rattle off a list along the lines of the above. If you plump for ice cream, she will say *Quel parfum?*, what flavour. Elaborate confections are rare, but *un chariot*, dessert trolley, might be wheeled in and *grand dessert* allows you free rein. *La tarte maison* in an ordinary restaurant may not be mentioned although it is available; it is bound to be a flat open apple tart, homemade, and is worth asking for.

9 Fruit

The fruit basket or *corbeille de fruits*, with fresh fruit in season, will be presented. By and large, dessert and fruit are amalgamated into one course. You may even have to decide between cheese and dessert/fruit.

Coffee is never included in the price of a meal. You will get a small black coffee if you order *un café*, white if you stipulate *un café crème*. (But *café au lait* means a large coffee with hot milk as drunk at breakfast, not ordinary white coffee.) It is mostly served by the cup, and you are charged for each refill.

Ordering

To attract the attention of the waiter or waitress, say *monsieur*, *madame* or *mademoiselle*, depending on appearance. *Garçon*, for waiter, is rarely heard nowadays.

When you have had a chance to study the menu before the meal, you will be asked if you have made up your mind — *Vous avez choisi?* You should then say that you would like *le menu à 40f* or whatever, and indicate your chosen starter and — *Pour suivre?* — main course to follow. Don't reject *le plat du jour* as yesterday's leftovers: it is on the contrary the chef's speciality of the day. You're not expected to choose the dessert at this

*"Un escargot, s'il vous plaît — un escargot simplement
pour regarder."*

[*A snail, please — a snail just to look at.*]

Drawing by P. Barlow; © 1961 The New Yorker Magazine. Inc.

stage. You will doubtless be wished *bon appétit* when
the food arrives, to which you should reply *Merci*, thank
you.

For the answer to the vital question, *Et comme
boisson?*, what will you have to drink, see p. 112. You
will probably be offered mineral water or *eau minérale*
automatically, but if you prefer ordinary water, which is
free, you can request *une carafe d'eau*.

Paying the bill   To pay the bill, ask for *l'addition, s'il vous plaît*. It
nearly always includes service charge and will say so —
STC, SC or *tout compris*. Otherwise you should add 15
per cent. Wine is sometimes thrown in with the price of
le menu; if it is, it will be indicated by *vin/boisson
compris*.

Le déjeuner, lunch, commences around noon and *le dîner*,   *Eating times*
about 7.30 to 8. Even in the south where they are
supposed to dine later, and in Paris, where they do, you
should get to a restaurant before 9 and start looking or
booking before 8. This applies particularly on Friday
and Saturday nights. Most restaurants stop serving lunch
by 2 at the latest, and dinner by 10.

Lunch still tends to be the main meal of the day,
often eaten out, and dinner a lighter affair taken at
home, starting inevitably with soup. You will soon
discover that the two-hour midday break is sacred in the
provinces, particularly when heat compels the habit as in
the Midi. But it's increasingly hard to generalize, for
Parisians and city dwellers are foresaking the long lunch.
And the chic alternative to the theatre is now dining out
in the evening. In any case, devotees of the lunchtime
picnic followed by dinner in a restaurant have no cause
for alarm: in most places you can fare just as splendidly
in the evening — except on Sundays. (Remember that in
Paris many restaurants close completely on Sundays.)

Then and on public holidays, the whole of France
goes out for a restaurant lunch. Don't let this deter you
from participating in one of the great French rituals, but
make sure you arrive early or book a table in advance —
réserver une table. Tables are never held if you're late. If
you're planning to arrive on a Sunday, it's important to
remember that many restaurants will be closed in the
evening, and those that are open may be offering only a
simple menu.

English schoolchildren are taught that the French keep   *Table*
the same knives and forks throughout a meal. No doubt   *manners*
it's one of those myths devised by perfidious Albion to
prove what barbarians the Frogs really are. In fact,
cutlery is plentiful at each course in restaurants and
most homes.

When you sit down, several plates are piled up in
front of you for the initial stages of the meal, and
whisked away as you finish each course. The supply is
exhausted when you reach the salad and new ones
appear. Soup is poured into a round flat plate and consumed with a tablespoon. It is not considered good
manners to transfer the fork to your right hand and
dispense with the knife — Americans please note.

However, fingers are OK as implements, especially

for dealing with shellfish, frogs' legs, snails, chicken joints, meat bones. No one will raise an eyebrow if you tuck your napkin into your collar before assaulting the seafood platter. But, in the very best circles, you would refrain from mopping up the juices with a piece of bread. You are supposed to put knife and fork in the 5 o'clock position on the plate, to indicate that you have finished.

The correct French posture, when not actively eating, is to have the wrists lightly resting on the table (not the elbows). This is to show that you have no weapons concealed under the table.

Bread is always provided and replenished, although not butter or side plates. For this reason, many restaurants have paper table-cloths and these are sometimes used by the waiter to add up your bill, and by great artists as doodling pads.

Don't forget that, in answer to a question, *s'il vous plaît* equals yes, and *merci* no.

Cuisine dégoutante or unmentionables   There is nothing cosmetic about French food. Fish, for instance, really looks like fish, whether in the market or on your plate, when head, eyes and tail are left|on; meat, even in the supermarket, comes in recognizable cuts instead of uniform, cellophane-wrapped steaks; chickens and rabbits can be bought alive.

One of the classic and favourite French dishes is *tête de veau vinaigrette*, calf's head with oil and vinegar dressing. *Tripes*, ox stomach, is another, cooked in various special ways all over France, notably in Caen and Lyon. Remnants which would be discarded in other nations can become culinary triumphs.

However, if you are sensitive about offal or variety meats, you should avoid *cervelles*, brains, *foie*, liver, *ris de veau*, calf's sweetbreads (not rice), *rognons*, kidneys and *rognons blancs*, a euphemism for testicles.

Many of the *charcuterie* products have unpleasant origins, although they are well disguised. *Andouilles* and *andouillettes* are sausages made with strips of pig's stomach and other bits, packed into intestines. *Hure* is brawn or pig's head. *Boudin noir* consists largely of pig's blood. Indeed, blood is sometimes used to thicken sauces, notably in *canard à la rouennaise*, Rouen-style duck, and *civet de lièvre*, stewed hare.

Horsemeat is popular in the north of France, where it

is best to avert the gaze from the horse-butcher's, but is not often knowingly encountered in restaurants. And those small birds like lark and thrush are thankfully rare. *Alouettes/oiseaux sans tête*, literally headless larks/birds, actually means beef or veal olives.

Frogs' legs, of course, are popularly associated with the French. But it is only the thighs or *cuisses de grenouilles* that are eaten, usually fried or in a sauce. They look and taste like chicken drumsticks, only, of course, much smaller.

Escargots, snails, are generally served piping hot in a garlicky sauce, six or twelve at a time. You hold the shell in a special snail clamp, extract the flesh with a long fork and suck up the juices. Snails are often described as *bourguignons*; a smaller variety is known as *petit gris*.

Garlic — *ail*, plural *aulx* — may be a hazard for some and, in the south, it's difficult to escape. French garlic can be mild and subtle and, if its staying power seems the same, at least you're in good company.

Drinking

In one respect at least the French live up to their image: they are still the world's heaviest drinkers. Consumption of wine in France is about 80 litres per head of population a year, compared with 70 in Italy, the next most bibulous nation, 25 in West Germany and a mere 8 in Britain.

But that other picture, of French babies being weaned on wine, is fading. One of the achievements of the government anti-alcohol drive has been to prohibit the serving of drinks to children under 14. Alcohol intake as a whole has certainly declined from the time, 25 years ago, when the French disposed of an annual 140 litres of wine each. It has also changed in complexion. Instead of consuming gut-rotting plonks and fire-waters, the French are turning to better wines, including Champagne. This is considered a fashionable tipple and *le scotch*, whisky, has become the smart aperitif. Beer sales have soared. Even the convention of having wine with every meal is on the wane, and mineral water or fruit juice is the chic alternative.

Nevertheless, alcoholism is a serious problem, particularly in Brittany and the north, and red wine is the major culprit. Something like three million men drink over a litre of this a day — not necessarily with harmful effects if they are involved in hard physical labour. Farmers and others are allowed to distil their own spirits, up to ten litres per annum for home use, but must now pay tax on it.

Wine You could easily accumulate a library of books on the subject of French wine, many of them heavy with the mystique and snobbery which surround it. This is not the place to discuss the details of *crus* and *cuvées*, *châteaux* and *climats*. For these, and information about the different wine regions, grape varieties, soil, methods of vinification, tasting, laying down and so on, please look elsewhere. But if you want to make the most of the wines of France, you might as well throw away your pocket vintage guide.

France produces around a quarter of the world's wine. *Types of wine* Total French output in 1982 was 79 million hectolitres (1 hectolitre = 100 litres). But less than a third of this represents the top quality wines, the big names of Burgundy, Bordeaux and elsewhere. The rest consists of table wines, which mostly stay in their own country.

About half of these originate in the Languedoc. Here thousands of peasant growers churn out vast amounts of mediocre wine and erupt in ferocious riots whenever they are threatened by falling prices or cheap Italian and Spanish imports. The official response is to pacify them with subsidies, guarantees and promises of protection.

At the same time, the government has encouraged the replacement of old vines with new and better ones. This leads to constant upgrading and expansion of the higher classes of wine, not always without a deterioration in standards. Production of *AC* wines (see below) has approximately doubled in ten years and the figure for 1982 was 19 million hectolitres.

There are four categories of wine in France.

AOC or *AC* (*appellation d'origine contrôlée*) wines are strictly regulated by a national body as to the grape variety used, method of production and maximum yield allowed and are made in a precisely defined area. This can range from a single vineyard, notably in Burgundy, to a larger overall district such as the Côtes du Rhône or Bordeaux. So, although wines with the *appellation d'origine contrôlée* carry an assurance of some merit, they cover a wide spectrum — embracing Le Montrachet, for instance, one of the finest and most expensive of white wines, and the basic red Beaujolais, designed for everyday drinking. Moreover, fears have been voiced that *AC* quality is being diluted by a few of the recent promotions to that status, which are deemed unworthy.

VDQS wines are governed by similar but less stringent requirements. These *vins délimités de qualité supérieure* are usually good value and can be excellent, especially since many are striving for the award of an *AC*. Corbières is a reliable example out of a large number.

Vins de pays are made from approved grape varieties in the region indicated by their name, for example Vin de Pays de l'Hérault. This rank is a fairly recent creation, to distinguish them from the mass of *vins de table*, which they generally deserve.

Vins de table, the biggest group by far, may be the result of blending from several areas or even countries. They are priced according to alcoholic strength and usually sold under brand names, like the well-known Nicolas. These are the cheapest wines, bought at the supermarket or wine cooperative, but they can still be quite palatable.

A wine label tells you which category the wine belongs to, the most important point, plus other relevant details. Don't be misled by statements like *mise en bouteilles dans nos caves*, bottled in our cellars, which can be totally meaningless. In fact, a château-bottled wine is not necessarily superior, for bottling might be carried out more efficiently by a large wine house.

AC, VDQS and *vin de pays* bottles usually contain 75 centilitres (25.36 US oz). *Vin de table* is available in litre bottles, increasingly made of plastic. The glass bottle with three stars stamped in it is *une bouteille consignée*, a returnable bottle, which you can take to any appropriate shop or supermarket and get a few centimes back.

How to read a wine list   In all but the grandest French restaurants, *la carte des vins* is a short and simple list of wines and other drinks. The wines tend to be arranged by region, starting with the local ones and then continuing through Bordeaux, Burgundy, Beaujolais, Rhône, Alsace, Loire, Champagne. Foreign wines, like German or Italian ones, are rare.

If you're in a wine-growing area, and it's hard *not* to be in France, the wisest policy is to concentrate on its products. In the Loire valley, say, you could try a red Chinon and a sweet white Coteaux du Layon, both reasonably priced in their own territory and not often seen outside it. A worthy *AC* wine retailing at 12f in the shops would be about 38f in a restaurant, which is still good value.

But any ideas of living off the finest clarets or Champagne are doomed to disappointment. These get an obligatory mention on most wine lists, but can be just as astronomical in francs as they are in dollars or sterling. In an ordinary restaurant, where their sole purpose is to add a touch of prestige, they will probably have been sitting around for ages in the wrong conditions. A better approach, and one which will earn more respect from the management, is to ignore the familiar but expensive names and venture into the wealth of regional wines.

In a smart establishment, of course, where the wine list may be more daunting, you should consult the *sommelier*, the wine waiter. He wears a badge of a bunch of grapes in his lapel and is there to advise.

Supposing you find yourself in a part of France which is relatively poor in local wines — Normandy, Brittany, the north or, indeed, Paris. Even here, there should be plenty of economical alternatives on the wine list. Sound reds from the Côtes du Rhône and Beaujolais have a fairly national distribution, as do whites like Muscadet and Bourgogne Aligoté. Look out for Cahors, and Pécharmant, one of the better reds from Bergerac; lesser wines like Côtes du Ventoux, Coteaux de Tricastin, Corbières, Minervois, Costières du Gard, Côtes du Roussillon, Côtes de Provence; and minor districts of Burgundy — Givry, Montagny, Mâcon, Côte de Beaune; or of Bordeaux — the Côtes de Blaye, Bourg and Castillon, Fronsac.

Incidentally, when staying in a hotel for several days, you can keep a bottle on the go. If you don't finish it at one meal, it will be recorked and brought out at the next.

House wines

Most restaurants have a house wine, invariably a local one which has been personally selected by the owner. Very often it is not mentioned on the wine list; if it is, it will be called *cuvée* or *réserve du patron* or *de la maison* and may even have an individual label on the bottle. It is a sensible choice and always good value.

Let observation be your guide — see what everyone else is drinking. When the carafe wine seems to be the popular thing, don't hesitate to inquire what it is. It may be fairly ordinary, but it will be better than the cheapest wines on the list, and probably cheaper.

You can ask for *une carafe*, which holds a litre, *une demi-carafe*, a half litre, or *un quart*, a quarter litre. Or it may be served in a *pichet*, a small jug. You can also order *un verre de vin*, a glass of wine.

A *menu* with *vin/boisson compris* means that the house wine is included in the price. Don't expect to be able to choose from the wine list.

Other alcoholic drinks

Apéritifs

Every French café boasts a bar stocked with a glittering array of bottles in all shapes, sizes and hues. Many of these contain the sweet and syrupy concoctions with which the French like to tickle their palates. Dubonnet is the best-known member of a large family of such aperitifs, generally wine-based and aromatic and sometimes with a bitterness imparted by quinine. They are often taken diluted with water or soda. Most go under brand names, like St Raphael, Picon, Ambassadeur, Lillet. *Un Byrrh* is what you might get if you meant to order a beer (*une bière*), but it's just palatable. Suze, made out of gentian roots, is to be avoided at all costs.

Vermouths, such as Noilly Prat, and Chambéry from the Alps, are drier in style. But sweet *porto* is popular and so are sweet wines, Banyuls and Montbazillac for instance, which others might consider more suitable for dessert. You might be given a sweet wine if you're invited into a French home for a pre-dinner drink, so be prepared.

Pineau des Charentes, a blend of Cognac and grape juice, is a speciality of the Cognac country. But you can request *un Kir* or *vin blanc cassis* anywhere in France, although this was a Dijon invention and should be made with the blackcurrant liqueur for which the town is famous, plus Aligoté, the dry white wine of Burgundy.

Anis and *pastis*, the aniseed and liquorice flavoured aperitifs, are common throughout France, particularly in the south. Pernod, Berger and Ricard are the major brands. This type of drink is always mixed with water, which turns it cloudy, and is a potent brew despite the suggestion of toothpaste. In fact, Pernod is a substitute for the lethal absinthe, banned in 1915.

Xérès, sherry, is not a regular drink. However, *le gin-tonic* is advancing and *le whisky* or *scotch* has super-seded\many of the traditional aperitifs. Imported drinks like these are expensive, which presumably gives them an extra cachet. If you want something with tonic, it is *avec Schweppes*, or with ice, *avec des glaçons*.

You can always order a glass of wine in a café. It will be a cheap and drinkable local one, or one with a wide distribution. Often it's Muscadet.

French people take their aperitifs in a café, rather than at home or in a restaurant before a meal. But a grandiose menu might offer *les amuse-gueule*, a little

'*The usual, Georges — one Guinness, two whiskies, four Coca-Colas, two Schweppes tonics, and give the English girl a Pernod.*'

Reproduced by courtesy of *Punch*

plate of shrimps, olives or other appetizers to nibble with your glass of Champagne.

Beer

For a nation of wine drinkers, the French consume a large, and increasing, amount of beer. It is brewed all over northern France. National names like Kanterbräu, Kronenbourg and Fischer/Pêcheur come from Alsace and Lorraine and are representative of the predominant lager type or *bière blonde*. However, some brown ale or *bière brune* is produced in Flanders and Artois.

Draught beer, *à la pression*, is available, but comes out of a keg. You can ask for *une bière pression* or *une pression*. Or order *un demi*, roughly equivalent to half a pint. A shandy is *un panaché* or *une bière limonade*.

Cider

Cider, by contrast, has not caught on to any significant extent; the fact that it costs more than wine does not help. As a normal drink, alone or with a meal, it is confined to the west and north of France, especially Normandy and Brittany.

Here, most of the cider is manufactured, either the pasteurized product of a factory or home-made *cidre de ferme*, which is more popular and therefore more expensive. In both cases, however, French rules are strict:

cider must be fermented from fresh apple juice, using the natural yeasts in the skins and without added sugar to determine the sweetness. Authentic cider is supposed to fizz only when poured into the glass, but it is usually described as *cidre bouché*, sparkling, and can be explosive when you unleash the Champagne-style cork of the bottle. The Vallée d'Auge has a reputation for the finest cider.

Digestifs

A *digestif* is a liqueur or spirit taken after the meal, allegedly to aid the digestion. As with aperitifs, the range is vast.

Cognac is the world's most celebrated brandy, but it would be a pity to miss its less familiar cousin, Armagnac, from further south in Gascony. Some maintain it has an earthier flavour. The top quality Cognac comes from districts close to the town of Cognac confusingly known as Grande and Petite Champagne. So, if you see the words Fine Champagne, they denote an excellent Cognac and have nothing to do with bubbly. *Fine* is actually the nearest term the French have for grape brandy. On labels it must be used in conjunction with the region of production, for example Fine Marne, brandy from the Marne. The only exceptions to this are Cognac and Armagnac. Therefore, *fine* on its own, or *fine maison*, the staple brandy of the establishment, should mean Cognac or Armagnac.

Calvados, the cider brandy, is a speciality of Normandy and the best, again, is from the Pays d'Auge. Ask for *un calva* if you want a glass of it. In a restaurant, the proprietor might try to tempt you with his ten-year-old bottle, but it's doubtful whether it justifies the price. Anyhow, you're safe from the rougher stuff, which is not allowed to call itself Calvados but must be known as *eau-de-vie de cidre*.

Eau-de-vie means a spirit distilled from fruit, cereals (e.g. gin, from grain) or other substances. In the case of *eau-de-vie de marc*, these consist of the grape skins, pips and stalks left behind after pressing the wine. The drink, generally abbreviated to *marc* and followed by a territorial name, like Marc de Bourgogne, can be very pungent.

Other *eaux-de-vie* are more refined, notably those for which Alsace is renowned. These colourless fruit brandies, also known as *alcools blancs*, include *kirsch*,

from cherries, and others named after the fruit concerned
— *mirabelle, quetsch*, both from plums, *framboise*, raspberry, *poire Williams*, pear.

Alcohols flavoured with fruit or other things are
produced on a local scale in many parts of France,
sometimes clear and bitter, more often sticky and
sweet, like the plum brandy or *prune* and the *eau de
noix*, of walnuts, from the Dordogne. *Genièvre*, Dutch-
style gin, is drunk in the north around Lille.

Crème de cassis, blackcurrant liqueur, is still associated
with Dijon, but other *crèmes, de menthe* (mint), *de
cacao* (cocoa) and so on, are common-place. France is
the home of the famous Bénédictine, from Fécamp in
Normandy, and Chartreuse, from the Alps. There are
many more in this genre, herbal and often distilled to a
secret recipe.

Soft drinks

Things like Coca Cola, Fanta, lemonade (*limonade*) are
easily obtainable in cafés and shops. Remember that
bottles of most fizzy drinks are returnable, and the shop
will give back your few centimes of deposit. Vittel
Délices and the unfortunate Pschitt are sparkling fruit
drinks.

If you order *un jus d'orange*, you should get real
orange juice from a bottle. It is expensive. So is *un
citron pressé*, freshly squeezed lemon juice to which you
add your own sugar, but deliciously refreshing. Milk
doesn't count as a drink in France, except for small
children, but you can always try asking for *un verre de
lait*.

There is also a collection of non-alcoholic and brightly
coloured *sirops*, all very sweet and usually diluted or
mixed with other drinks. The vivid red *grenadine* is
derived from pomegranate. *Un diabolo-menthe*, lemonade
with mint cordial, looks grown-up but is innocuous.

Water

The impurity of French tap water used to provide the
perfect excuse for sticking to wine (and even cleaning
one's teeth in it). Today, water from taps is generally
safe to drink and you can order a glass or jug of ordinary
water in a restaurant (see p. 106). But never drink from a
tap labelled *eau non potable* (not drinking water).

A glass of water is always brought when you order ice
cream in a café. And a flask accompanies a Pernod, so
that you can spin it out ad infinitum.

The French are very keen on mineral water and drink a lot more of it than other nations. There's a huge assortment of *eaux minérales*, both sparkling and still, and many of them claim to be therapeutic, particularly for the kidneys. They can be quite pricey, even more so when in individual bottles. Ask for *un Perrier* in a café and it will probably cost more than a glass of wine.

Over 1,000 springs in France are officially registered and their water classified on a similar pattern to the wine categories *AC*, *VDQS* and *vin de pays*. These are *eau minérale naturelle*, about 50 in number and rigidly controlled, *eau de source* and *eau de table*.

Hot drinks

Tea always comes neat in France, unless you specify *thé au lait/au citron*, tea with milk/lemon. Similar problems arise with coffee (see p. 105). Apart from these hot chocolate (*chocolat*) is quite common, especially at breakfast.

Tisanes (same word in French) are an after-dinner alternative, which are believed to be healthful. These are infusions or herbal teas, like *tilleul*, lime flower, *verveine*, verbena, *camomille*, camomile, and *menthe*, mint.

How to buy wine

Buying in shops

Wine is sold in grocery shops, supermarkets and hypermarkets. Wine merchants and wine shops as such scarcely exist and where they do, in large towns, they generally cater for a snob trade.

Even the little grocer's on the corner stocks a basic selection of wines, and the choice at the super- or hypermarket seems limitless. But regional products again are very much to the fore, together with standards like Beaujolais and Muscadet. As with the wine list in a restaurant, you will get better value by sticking with these rather than hovering over the first-growth clarets.

Champagne, sadly, falls within the same price bracket, despite bumper harvests in 1982 and 1983. But there are some worthy competitors, namely Saumur blanc, made by the same method as Champagne, and Blanquette de Limoux, as well as the cheap fizzy wines with no pretensions to be the real thing. Shopping for wine is an opportunity to try something more unusual, for instance the *vins doux naturels* or *muscats* like Frontignan and Beaumes de Venise, which are sweet fortified wines.

In general, you tend to get the best range and value from the supermarket. It very often has a special-offer wine too, which could be a bargain. But you will be surprised by the parochialism of France: all the wines of the locality may be there on the shelves, but nothing from the neighbouring district 'over the border'.

Most French people buy their wine direct from the source. There is every encouragement for you to do the same, evident as soon as you enter a wine-growing area. Signs proclaiming *vente directe/détail*, direct/retail sales, and *dégustation et vente*, tasting and sales, are everywhere. In Alsace they say *propre récolte*, meaning literally that the grower is selling wines made from his own harvest, in other words from grapes of his land. *Buying direct and visiting vineyards*

Why, you may wonder, are rose trees planted at the end of the rows of vines, particularly in Bordeaux? Being more susceptible to blight than the grapes, their original purpose was to act as an advance detector of the disease. Now they are there for show and the vines are sprayed blue with copper sulphate to ward off mildew.

The prestigious names of the wine trade are well geared to receive the tourist. The great Champagne houses in Rheims and Epernay and the famous shippers in Cognac are the most thoroughly regimented, offering conducted tours of their premises in several languages.

In Burgundy, Beaune, the headquarters of many wine merchants, is a good starting point. Its tourist office will guide you in the right direction for visitable vineyards. Alternatively, you can just follow the signposted *route des grands crus* (literally, road of the great growths, or finest vineyards) through the heart of Burgundy, the Côte d'Or, stopping wherever the fancy takes you. One of the most highly organized properties there is the Château de Meursault: for an entrance fee, you can enjoy a long wine-tasting session as you progress through the cellars where, such is the variety on offer, you have to spit it out in the approved manner to remain sober. At the end, there is the unspoken assumption that you will buy, but no obligation to do so. Unless you're prepared to pay almost as much as you would at home, it's better to regard such a visit as educational and then continue to one of the less obvious establishments for actual purchases. Here too you may be led through the vats and bottles before sampling a glass or two, but more informally and often by the owner himself. This makes it embarrassing if you decide not to buy anything. He

probably won't speak English either. Associations of
growers usually offer good value, so look out for signs
like *cave coopérative* and *union des viticulteurs.*

Much the same applies to Bordeaux now, though here
the wine-makers go in more for guided tours, at places
like Château Lafite and Château Margaux. For information, you could begin at the town's tourist office or
inquire at one of the numerous information centres,
known as *maisons du vin* and *syndicats viticoles*, throughout the region. Their staff can also arrange appointments
for visits to the exclusive Château d'Yquem and Château
Mouton-Rothschild. Otherwise, letters of introduction
are no longer necessary in Bordeaux and you can simply
turn up at most of the châteaux. Again you get the best
value, in terms of buying wine, from one of the many
cooperatives.

Don't forget that wine properties all over France
often close for lunch and sometimes at weekends.

Bottles of wine bought direct from the grower like
this are not necessarily much cheaper than in a shop,
although there's usually a quantity discount for buying
over a dozen. The advantage is that you can taste before
you pay and be assured of the quality of the product.

Buying in bulk   The way to make real savings is to buy unbottled or
loose wine, known as *en vrac*, and the place to do so is
the growers' cooperative or *cave coopérative. AC* wines
can be as little as 10f per litre and *vins de table* a mere
3f. The more you have, the cheaper it is; but there's no
reason why you shouldn't take along a single litre
bottle to be filled.

You do have to supply your own containers; but
most cooperatives will sell you *une bonbonne plastique*,
a plastic demijohn of about 5 litres capacity, or *un
cubitainer*, a collapsible plastic cube with tap inside a
cardboard box (like a wine box), holding from 10 to 20
litres. For really big purchases, you will need *un fût* or
tonnelet plastique, a plastic cask or barrel. The snag is
that all these, including the *cubitainer*, are designed for
transport and not the storage of wine. You must bottle
your own, and as quickly as possible.

These extras, of course, increase the basic cost of the
wine. Nevertheless, Britons might be tempted to import
in bulk and, with excise duty at present about £1 a
bottle, it can be worth it. In theory, you can buy wine

free of French tax, if it is intended solely for export. But this involves a lot of hassle, particularly at customs where you will be relegated to the slow-moving commercial queue with the lorries. Plonk never tastes quite the same when you get it home, unfortunately.

But, in any case, whenever you buy bulk wine, you must obtain from the supplier *un acquit*. This is a transport certificate, which will be filled in with the details of your journey home, even if you live in France and it's only a few miles. The certificate is required by law for the carriage of wine through France, whether by French residents or foreigners.

Shopping for Food

Calling early at the bakery to pick up a fresh loaf still warm from the oven, choosing a big crinkly lettuce in the market, tasting morsels of cheese before you select — food shopping in France is not a chore but an entertainment.

Everything is conducted on an intimate level. As you step into a shop or go up to a market stall, you will be greeted with the habitual *Bonjour m'sieurs-dames*, not only by the shopkeeper but often by the other customers. Service is personal, with plenty of time for chat; purchases are individually and beautifully wrapped; and, when it comes to paying, there is the inevitable question, *Vous n'avez pas de la monnaie?*, have you got the right change, for the French seem to have great difficulty with all their little centimes. But in this, as in the whole transaction, there's no need to hurry.

This is an idealized picture, of course, and you will only fit into it if you speak the language. Nevertheless, even if your French vocabulary is limited to good morning and thank you, you can participate. Shopkeepers are generally understanding and cooperative with ignorant foreigners, and quite a lot can be achieved by signs and pointing, particularly as so much is on display. They will be less helpful if you take ages making up your mind, insist on tasting all the cheeses and then come away with 50 grammes of Gruyère. It all hinges on mutual respect.

Many grocers' stores have in fact become semi-self-service and therefore more anonymous. Others have turned into fully fledged supermarkets. Both will be welcome to the timid visitor.

Opening times Most food shops open at 8 in the morning or earlier, close at 12 noon, reopen in the afternoon at 2.30 or 3 and finally shut at 7 or 8 in the evening. This applies from Tuesday to Saturday. On Sundays and public holidays, they usually open in the morning. (For hypermarket times, see p. 131).

Markets happen in the morning, from 8 until 12. They take place once or twice a week, frequently a Saturday, in most towns. You can find out the local market days and the site, from the tourist office. Some places have a market hall with permanent stalls, which are open most of the week.

A baker's van may call daily in remote villages, and a mobile grocer or butcher once or twice a week. They usually honk to advertise their arrival.

Shop talk

Apart from the obligatory *bonjour* and *au revoir* to the shopkeeper. you should have various key phrases up your sleeve. For a start, how much is that — *C'est combien ça?*

The answer to the assitant's query, *Vous désirez?*, what would you like, is *Je voudrais*, I would like, whatever it is; or it could be *Je regarde*, I'm just looking. You're bound to be asked *Et avec ça?*, anything else, and *C'est tout?*, is that all?

Many things can be bought by pointing, for instance, *Un comme ça*, one like that, or by number — *six croissants*, *deux escalopes*. In the butcher or fishmonger, you can specify the number of people, *pour quatre personnes* (for four people) perhaps. You can request *une tranche*, a slice of ham or pâté, or *un morceau*, a piece, of cheese. *Ça suffit* is 'that's enough', and *Ça va*, fine.

However, there's no escaping the metric system, particularly in the fruit and veg. department. It was obviously designed for big families: *un kilo de cerises* is a lot of cherries, over 2 lb. Presumably because of this the French have also retained the old-fashioned *livre* or pound which, in current usage, equals half a kilo. For those more versed in imperial weights, the most useful quantities are *un demi-kilo*, or *cinq cents grammes* (½ kg or 500 g), just over 1 lb; *deux cents grammes* (200 g), 7–8 oz; and *cent grammes* (100 g), just under 4 oz.

If you're buying a present for someone, a selection of chocolates maybe, tell the assistant *C'est pour offrir*. It will then be specially gift wrapped.

Shops

La boulangerie (baker)

A nineteenth-century French law enacted that every town and village over a certain size should have *une boulangerie* or *un dépôt de pain*. Thankfully the latter, merely shops selling bread, are far outnumbered by the former, where bread is baked twice a day on the premises. You can also get bread from the supermarket — not recommended.

Quality does vary from one bakery to the next, simply because the bread is home baked, so it's worth shopping around. Most bakers open early, including Sunday mornings, and remain open until about 8; and, while many close on Mondays, you should be able to find one open in any town on that day.

The price of bread is officially regulated and clearly displayed in the bakery as are the loaves themselves. The *baguette*, the archetypal French loaf or French stick, is always popular and you can ask for *une baguette* by name, or even *une demi-baguette*, a half. Apart from this — and you can point if you prefer — there is the thinner *ficelle*, and the fatter *pain*, the sort usually served in a restaurant in thick slices. *Pain demie*, soft rather than crusty, is the nearest equivalent to sandwich bread.

French bread doesn't keep, which is part of its charm and one of the reasons why no one has imitated it successfully outside France (the other being the type of flour used). However, if you do need a loaf that will last more than a day, try the huge round *pain de campagne*, or the *pain de seigle*, rye bread.

Brown bread is slowly advancing, even in the land of the *baguette*. Some bakers give a nod to fashion with *pain complet/intégral*, whole-meal bread, or *pain au son*, bread with added bran.

The bakery is also the place to buy *croissants, brioches* and *pains au chocolat*, collectively known as *viennoiseries*. *Une brioche* is a sort of rich bun, and *un pain au chocolat* a sweet light pastry with a little chocolate in the middle. Sometimes other buns and biscuits and local specialities are sold, and very often ice creams.

Surprisingly, you might think, France has launched its own 'real bread' campaign. About 700 bakers are member of the Association Qualité Pain and produce *une bagette* (sic) by traditional methods, which is said to recapture the original crustiness and flavour of the true *baguette*.

La pâtisserie
(cake-shop)   This is sometimes combined with the bakery, so it's hard to avoid those mouthwatering éclairs and choux buns and strawberry tartlets. Everything, including the elaborate cakes, is homemade, delicious and expensive.

Croissants au beurre, a richer, sweeter version of the baker's made with butter, are sold here as well. Many cake-shops sell homemade ice cream, which costs more than the well-known brands like Miko and Gervais.

The *pâtisserie* is busiest on a Sunday morning, when the French like to buy in the dessert for a meal at home. They very rarely make such things themselves.

This may well be part of the cake-shop too. It is nothing as vulgar as a sweet-shop, but a confectioner's in the real sense of the word, specializing in hand-made chocolates and sweets, and possibly jams and preserved fruits — a luxury shop with prices to match.

La confiserie (confectioner)

If you are planning a picnic, the foregoing are merely diversions on the way to that emporium of al fresco foods, the *charcuterie*. It is not difficult to find, for even small villages seem to have one, usually in league with the butcher.

La charcuterie (delicatessen)

Technically a pork butcher, dealing in all the products of the pig, it tends to be like a delicatessen, stocked with a wide range of pies, quiches, pizzas, salads and ready-prepared dishes. However, you will save yourself francs by sticking to the simpler offerings and ignoring the dainty vol-au-vents. Things are labelled and on display, so you can point if necessary.

Saucisson sec or *à l'ail* (salami or garlic sausage), cold *rôti de porc* or *de boeuf* (roast pork or beef), *jambon blanc* (cooked ham), all make fine picnic fodder. These may be bought by the slice. Pâté normally comes in two main types — *pâté de campagne*, of pork, rough and garlicky, and *pâté de foie*, of liver, smooth and bland. An acceptable amount to ask for is 100 grammes, of these and also of the made-up salads.

For the adventurous cook, there are various sausage-type things to try: *saucisse, boudin, andouillette* can all be grilled. The *charcuterie* may also sell fresh pork and something called *chair*, literally flesh but in fact a kind of sausage meat.

Un traiteur, often absorbed into the *charcuterie*, is a caterer who prepares made-up dishes for home consumption, as well as wedding feasts and banquets. You can take your own casserole round to have it filled with *poulet chasseur* or *sauté de veau* and no one would guess it didn't come from your own oven.

La rôtisserie may also be an adjunct to the *charcuterie*. This is where joints of meat, chickens and so on are spit-roasted before your eyes. Like the cake shop, it does a brisk trade on Sunday mornings.

La boucherie
(butcher)

Many visitors to France will never go into the butcher's shop, either because they think it's easier to buy their meat in a supermarket or because they're not cooking for themselves. But a good butcher is the quintessence of the French shopkeeper who prides himself on personal service to his customers. He will dice and trim stewing steak for a *boeuf bourguignon*, and automatically throw in a bit of salt pork as well; he will mince veal for a terrine; he will roll a shoulder of lamb for roasting; he will joint a chicken for a *coq au vin*.

The butcher sells the usual kinds of meat — beef, veal, lamb but not always pork — and, normally, poultry and game. However, the latter sometimes have their own shop, *un volailler* (poulterer's), and are also obtainable in markets and supermarkets.

French cuts of meat, especially beef and veal, are different from British and American: French butchers cut with the grain rather than across it. Prime joints and secondary ones alike are meticulously prepared, so there is much less wastage in terms of fat and bone. You could attempt to master words like *faux-filet* and *sous-noix*, but there is really no need and generally no exact equivalent. Instead, you should tell the butcher what you want to cook or what type of meat and method of cooking, and for how many people. You can see what you're getting, as it's clearly labelled and priced, and may even have the name of a dish attached, like *pot-au-feu*. Obviously it helps here to know some French, but a little advance investigation with a dictionary should be enough for anyone with even the most basic knowledge of the language.

Bifteck is a loose expression for steak and one which is best avoided. *Bifteck haché* is mince or hamburger. *Mouton* is the general term for the meat of a young sheep, the same as lamb in English, and doesn't mean an elderly animal; *agneau*, on the other hand, refers to real lamb, possibly milk fed, *de lait*, or reared on salt meadows, *pré-salé*, and therefore expensive. If you like crackling on your roast pork in the English style, you will be disappointed, since the skin is removed.

Unless you go to *une boucherie chevaline*, horse-butcher's, by mistake — difficult as it's identified by a model of a horse's head — there's no risk of ending up with horsemeat. Similar to beef, it's much the same price.

Even a French chicken looks and tastes different, particularly if it's *un poulet fermier/de grain*, free range/corn fed or, best of all, a Poulet de Bresse with its own *appellation* (see p. 98). Battery birds are increasingly common, but usually fresh rather than frozen. Whole chickens are sold with head and feet intact, unless you ask for them to be removed. Giblets, on the other hand, are seldom included. You can always request *la moitié*, half, or *le quart*, quarter, of a chicken.

Don't dismiss exotic alternatives such as *pintade*, guinea fowl, and *cailles*, quails, on grounds of cost: they can be quite reasonable. French, not Chinese, rabbit is also widely available. Wild rabbit is *lapin de garenne*.

The quality of meat and poultry in France, plus the copious supply of good cheap wine, opens up whole new horizons for the cook. Because everything is so beautifully prepared, you can make the most of secondary cuts in stews, lengthily simmered and better still when re-heated. And, provided you have a stove and a solid saucepan, a genuine *boeuf en daube* (beef stew) tastes even finer on a campsite.

Fishmongers are less common than other shops, but the fish stall is a standard feature of markets and fresh fish is often sold at supermarkets. The variety is staggering and recognizably fishy, sometimes alive, but distinctly foreign. Identifying what you want is a problem. The fish are usually labelled and priced but, unless you have an excellent dictionary, this won't get you very far. It's certainly easier if you have enough French to ask advice, plus a dash of culinary confidence.

La poisson-nerie (fishmonger)

However, mussels may be familiar to some, and these are excellent value. Oysters too are relatively cheap. *Ecrevisses*, a sort of freshwater prawn, are reasonably priced, but must be bought and cooked alive. Monkfish, *lotte* or sometimes *baudroie*, is priced according to its new-found esteem, but it's very good and there's no waste. Another ubiquitous fish both on stalls and in restaurants is *merlan*, whiting. But there is little point in asking for fresh cod, *cabillaud*, which is rare; however, in a salted state, *morue*, it's quite common.

In the north and west such luxuries as sole and turbot (same words in French) seem more accessible than on the English side of the Channel. Baby sole or *céteaux* come from the Atlantic coast and can be fried as they are. *Truite saumonée*, salmon trout (or it might just be big trout with pink flesh) is a good buy. If you thought sardines (same word) and anchovies (*anchois*) only came in tins, this is the time to try them fresh. They are delicious, and easy to cook, grilled over an open fire. Fresh tuna or *thon* is often available and may be purchased by the slice.

You can ask to have fish cleaned and gutted (*vider*), or filleted (*découper en filets*), or the heads removed (*enlever les têtes*).

L'épicerie or l'alimentation générale (grocer) The grocer's store is also a dairy, wine shop and, very often, greengrocer. It will probably be semi-self-service, that is you grab a trolley (*un chariot*) and help yourself, queuing only at the cheese counter and for fruit and vegetables.

As well as the obvious things, this is the place to buy coffee: be sure to get *moulu*, ground, unless you have a grinder. (see also p. 132.)

Here you have the chance to browse among the cheeses of the refrigerated display — commercialized Camemberts and goat's-milk cheeses and prepacked Roquefort — but still instructive in their variety. You will come across delicacies like Petits Suisses, to be eaten with jam or strawberries or other fruit, *fromage blanc*, which is a sort of cross between cream cheese and yoghourt, and a host of different yoghourts.

Not all French dairy produce is pasteurized. *Lait cru*, raw or untreated milk, lasts for a day only and must be boiled before use. In practice, most French people buy long life or UHT milk. Milk is graded into red top — full cream, blue top — skimmed, and green top — no fat or 0 per cent. *Crème fraîche* is not fresh cream in the English sense (no such thing exists in France), but is more akin to thick rich cream with a faintly sour flavour.

Butter (*le beurre*) is generally *doux*, unsalted, and occasionally *demi-sel*, slightly salted. Both kinds are expensive, the latter in particular. You can often buy butter unwrapped from a great block in the market, and this may be cheaper.

The cheese counter itself can be fairly limited. There

are usually hard cheeses like Gruyère and Cantal, both
suitable for cooking, and a big round Brie. The market is
a better place to track down and taste the local cheeses;
or of course *une fromagerie*, a proper cheese shop, if
there is one. When choosing a Camembert or similar
cheese, ask for it *pas fait*, unripe, or *fait*, ripe. It's quite
all right to test it yourself with a gentle prod of the
finger.

The grocery will probably charge a franc or two for
un sac, a carrier bag. But you can usually find empty
cartons (same word) near the entrance, to which you
may help yourself free, or one will be provided on
request.

Fruit and vegetables can be bought at most grocer's
shops and at the supermarket. There are very few
individual greengrocers, though you sometimes see
signs for *fruitier*, fruit-seller, or *primeurs*, fruit and veg.,
literally early ones.

*Les fruits and
les légumes
(fruit and
vegetables)*

In fruit-growing regions such as the Loire valley, you
can get peaches or nectarines by the tray direct from the
farmer; or in the Dordogne, walnuts by the sack. But for
the finest selection, you should go to the market.

The core of the French market (*le marché*) is a caravan
of lorries which, when not mobile, convert into stalls
with umbrellas and awnings. The same market may do
the rounds of a district, calling at a different town each
day and probably finishing in the most important on
Saturday. The fringe consists of gnarled country folk,
who bring in minute amounts of home-grown vegetables,
tubs of honey from their beehives, or a few dozen eggs
and a clutch of live chickens.

*Le marché
(the market)*

There may be stalls of hardware and pots and pans;
china, including plain white plates and coffee bowls;
dresses, jeans and hats; nighties and fierce corsets; cheap
footware and espadrilles; flowers and plants; and, invariably and incongruously, two very black men selling
leather belts, bags and sandals and ethnic brass bangles.
In their case, you should haggle over the ludicrous
prices and might manage a bargain.

But the chief justification for the market is its fresh
produce. Crowning the fish and poultry, the cheese and
sausages, are the fruit and vegetables. They are a beautiful sight, not in the conventional sense perhaps, for the

French don't believe that big and unblemished equals
better, but for their sheer profusion and diversity.

You can choose from six or more different types of
salad green, from the familiar *romaine*, cos lettuce, to
the faintly bitter *scarole* or the quaintly named *pissenlit*,
dandelion leaves (supposed to have diuretic properties).
Tomatoes come in at least two guises — the ridged
Marmande or the soft plum kind. Potatoes can be
yellow and waxy, excellent for salads, red or dark violet;
beans can be green, purple or yellow, smooth or bumpy.

Some vegetables have a natural tag of origin — baby
turnips and carrots still with their feathery tops, tied
together in bunches; *courgettes*, zucchini, with their
orange flowers. Mangetout peas. where you eat the pod
and all, are common. Leeks are pencil thin and celery is
a darker green.

Vegetables that are rare treats elsewhere are common-
place in France — Swiss chard or seakale beet (*blettes*)
with fat white ribs, delicate pinkish shallots (*échalotes*),
fleshy *cèpes* and *chanterelles* from the fungus family.
You see women buying kilos of artichokes: the large
round sort are from Brittany, the smaller thin ones,
which can be eaten whole when young, from Provence.
Asparagus is plentiful in May and June; and it's worth
trying the thick white variety which the French rate
more highly than the commoner green type.

The range of fruit is just as breathtaking, particularly
in the summer when you have to make up your mind
between white fleshed peaches or nectarines, Charentais
or Canteloupe melons, cherries or strawberries. Only
the big red apples and infamous *goldens* (Golden
Delicious) lower the tone, although Reinettes, similar to
Coxes, are excellent.

Little is imported, so things like bananas and oranges,
if you do find them, are expensive. Everything is seasonal
too, and you won't be able to buy strawberries at in-
flated prices in the middle of winter.

All the fruit and vegetables are displayed and normally
labelled with the price per kilo, and there's really no
need to know the names. You are generally expected to
choose your own and hand them over to be weighed.
It's essential to take a bag.

Paris has many street markets which can cut the cost
of living in the capital. Two of the most popular are in
rue Mouffetard and rue de Buci.

General Shopping

It is no longer exceptional to find a hypermarket attached to a French town. Most of these huge supermarkets have been banished to the outskirts, where land is cheap with plenty of room for car parking. They're sometimes difficult to track down and often poorly signposted, deliberately one suspects. The locals may give the impression they don't want to direct you to their giant undercutting rival.

Le hypermarché or le hyper (hypermarket)

Prices are in fact lower at the hypermarket. This is one of its attractions for the French, who tend to do a weekly shop there. For the visitor, it has the extra bonus of anonymity, since you don't have to communicate with anyone.

Hypermarkets have all sorts of other advantages. They are generally open on Mondays, if only for the afternoon, when ordinary food shops are closed. On most other days they stay open until 10 at night. (Smaller ones might close for lunch and all are shut on Sundays.) They often accept credit cards (as do some supermarkets now). You pay at *la caisse*, checkout, or leave by the exit marked *sortie sans achats* in the unlikely event of coming away empty-handed. *En réclame* means that the article in on special offer, and there are always plenty of those.

The stock, of course, is enormous, and foreigners will be pleasantly surprised by its high quality. Shutting your ears to the canned music, you can lose yourself for hours amid the cheeses and wines. There is the additional convenience of having everything under one roof, not just food and drink of every description, but household goods and toiletries, kitchenware, china, electrical items, gardening equipment, do-it-yourself (*bricolage*), furniture, clothes, shoes and usually a cafeteria.

There are now over 400 hypermarkets in France and, as they become more acceptable, so they advance towards the centre of towns. Carrefour, one of the first, is still among the biggest and best. The Auchan chain also has a good reputation.

Best buys to take home

To many a motorized Briton on holiday, the hypermarket is above all the place to do last-minute shopping and stocking up. Indeed, you can take daytrips across the Channel for that sole purpose — as do an estimated 30,000 a day in the months before Christmas.

The object of the exercise is to buy things that are either cheaper inside France or virtually unobtainable outside it. Everyone will have their own ideas, but the following are some suggestions, together with alternative sources where these are better than the hypermarket. If you are equipped with a portable cool box, so much the better, though this in itself is quite a good buy in France.

Perishables

Cheese: hard types travel better, but Camembert is often sold unripe; goat's-milk cheese is risky, especially as most of it is unpasteurized; Petits Suisse, *fromage blanc*, *crème fraîche*, if you've acquired a taste for them.

Butter: expensive but delicious.

Pork products, cooked meats (*charcuterie*): salami-type sausage lasts for ages and there are usually several on special offer; ham is a bit dubious; pâtés and preserved meats (*confits*) are safer in tins.

Meat: continental cuts; veal — but not advisable even with a cool box and, like *charcuterie*, not encouraged by customs (see p. 19).

Fish and shellfish: difficult unless you can rush it home; better from a fish market at the port, especially live oysters and mussels packed in seaweed.

Bread: never succeeds, although you could try a huge *pain de campagne* with keeping qualities.

Fruit and vegetables

Anything that seems exotic and/or good value, probably best from the market. In particular, garlic — a bargain and looks nice in strings; shallots; artichokes; melons — choose them under-ripe; peaches, nectarines, plums — by the tray; herbs, fresh and dried — especially saffron and green pepper which are relatively reasonable.

Non-perishables

Coffee: can be half the price charged in the UK; buy *en grains*, beans, and keep in the fridge or freezer when you get home for longer life; Arabica and

Robusta are varieties of bean, the former considered more aromatic, the latter stronger.

Instant coffee (*café soluble*): not especially cheap, but for those who loathe the stuff there are two Nescafés that come close to real coffee and are not available in the UK — Spécial Filtre and Pur Arabica.

Jam: lot of flavours and without additives (must be kept in the fridge once opened) in attractive re-usable jars; fruit preserved in alcohol and pretty bottles; honey, particularly from the market.

Mustard: tremendous range, including Moutarde de Meaux in earthenware pots.

Vinegar: numerous varieties and flavours — wine, sherry, cider, raspberry, tarragon, rosemary, etc.

Oil: olive oil in big bargain tins or bottles — *vierge* is top quality; walnut or hazelnut oil.

Tins: tiny peas (*petits pois*), French beans (*haricots verts*); anchovies, sardines; snails; made-up dishes like *cassoulet.*

Packets: soups, especially Liebig brand; stocks, bouillons, etc. in great variety; pulses like lentils (*lentilles de Puy* are much esteemed); semolina (*couscous*, for the north African dish of the same name); dried fungi, especially *cèpes*.

Biscuits: all the lovely shapes like *palmiers, cigarettes, madeleines* — often cheaper in big tins.

Chocolate and sweets: eating chocolate (*chocolat à croquer*) bars are cheaper than in the UK and often on special offer; the same applies to chocolate Menier, supposedly for cooking. From the confectioner's (*confiserie*) buy luxury hand-made chocolate truffles, fresh *marrons glacés*. Beware of *dragées*, which should be sugared almonds, the type with a hard coating and whole nut inside, but can turn out to be soft-centred and quite different.

Drinks

Wines: from the medium price range (see p. 118).

Local spirits and liqueurs: e.g. Calvados, *crème de cassis*.

Mineral water: bulky but much cheaper.

Beer: ridiculously cheap — customs allowance is up to 50 litres per person.

Fruit syrups: if the children are addicted.

For the handyman and gardener, there's usually an

imaginative range of tools and equipment. Bathroom fittings and wallpapers are worth investigation. French watering cans are oval with a large rose, an effective design that actually pours rather than dribbles. You may be enticed by the seed packets — vegetables like *mâche*, lamb's lettuce, and *blette*, Swiss chard or seakale beet, that can just as easily be cultivated in the UK but are not so widely available. Decorative flower pots can be good value. Garden furniture — folding chairs, trestle tables — is excellent and cheap. Barbecues| cost less than in Britain. Plants like bay trees can be relatively reasonable, especially from the market, or else from the nursery (*pépinière*), but may be troublesome at customs.

For the cook, saucepans are a bit cheaper, which can save quite a lot if you're thinking of a Le Creuset casserole. Plain white china, glass tumblers and pottery are often available, but steer clear of anything labelled *liste des noces*, wedding list, which is generally hideous and expensive. French cookbooks are fascinating if you're up to the language.

Although books are about the same price as in the UK, maps and guides like the Michelin series are cheaper on the spot. Stationery — note pads, paper and so on — is less expensive, but envelopes are inferior in quality.

Electrical goods such as coffee makers, food processors and hair dryers can be worthwhile. But you must check the voltages first.

Toys are unusual, but not necessarily cheap.

Skiers should look into prices of French-made skis and boots.

Other shops

Opening times

Non-food shops open later, about 9 or 9.30, but otherwise keep similar hours. They are seldom open on Sundays, but usually on Monday afternoons.

La droguerie

Basically a hardware store, this is the place for all those essentials like detergent, plastic bowls, garbage bags, brushes, lightbulbs, tin openers and corkscrews. You can get camping gaz and replacement cylinders of butane gas, paint, weedkillers, and *une bombe insecticide*, insecticide, a vital requirement in the summer.

It also sells ordinary pots and pans, plates and cups and cutlery, as well as personal items such as soap, shampoo, combs.

This is very much an ironmonger's, specializing in metal objects — nails, screws, drills, tools.	*La quin-caillerie*

Here you can buy beauty preparations, cosmetics, scents *La parfumerie* and luxury toiletries. Cheaper to go to the *droguerie* or supermarket; better still to have bought them at home, even French brands.

This usually sells soap and so on, but is mainly for *La pharmacie* medical products (see p. 33).

Not necessarily a photographer's studio, though it might *Photographe* be, but a shop selling films and photographic equipment. *and photo-* You can also often find films at the tobacconist's. *graphie*

The tobacconist's, with its red cigar sign outside (this is *Le tabac* what it's supposed to represent), is a strange mix of officialdom and social club. In addition to stamps, it usually sells postcards, souvenirs, films and other odd-ments, and tends to be combined with a newsagent's or stationer's, a bar or café. It is also *le bureau de tabac*, the only authorized outlet for the sale of tobacco and cigarettes, which are a state monopoly. (A lot of tobacco is grown within France, in the south-west around Bergerac, where there is a museum devoted to it.) Most tobacconists stock the major American and British brands, and French imitations of these. The authentic Gauloise type are the cheapest. Ask for *un paquet*, a pack or packet, not 20.

The bookshop (*librairie*, as opposed to *la bibliothèque*, *La librairie* library) is often a stationer's (*papeterie*) as well; it may *and la* be a newsagent too, with the sign *journaux* or news- *papeterie* papers.

    Foreign newspapers, notably the *International Herald Tribune* and *Daily Telegraph*, are generally available in tourist areas. In such places you may find a limited selection of English-language books. These cost about 50 per cent more than the original price. Paris has several English bookshops, including a branch of W.H. Smith, and two English libraries.

Grands magasins or department stores were invented by **Department or** the French with the opening of Bon Marché on the Left **chain stores** Bank in Paris in 1852. It was followed by Galeries

Lafayette and Au Printemps, both on the boulevard Haussman, together with the more recent Marks & Spencer. Cheaper stores in the capital are La Samaritaine near the Pont Neuf and the Bazar de l'Hôtel de Ville. The most expensive is Aux Trois Quartiers in the boulevard de la Madeleine.

At these you can get just about everything you would expect from a department store. For multiple purchases ask for *un carnet d'achats* so that you can pay for everything together before you leave. They will also deliver to your hotel or the airport.

Opening times are roughly 9.30 to 6.30 from Monday to Saturday, often with late-night opening until 10 p.m. one day a week.

The chain stores like Monoprix and Prisunic are their paler reflections; both are actually subsidiaries of Galeries Lafayette and Au Printemps. They are similar to a good quality Woolworths in the UK and stock a wide range of budget articles.

Services

Laundry and cleaning

Dry cleaning, known as *le nettoyage à sec*, is carried out at an establishment under the sign *pressing*, literally steam ironing, or at *le teinturier*, literally someone involved in dyeing. It is expensive, particularly by American standards. Most *pressings* also do laundry — sheets, shirts and so on.

Washing can be more of a problem, unless you have access to the facilities of a well-equipped campsite or property. Since at least three-quarters of the population own a washing machine, launderettes or laundromats are few and far between, except in Paris. Inquire at the tourist office for the nearest *laverie automatique* or look in the phone directory.

Shoe repairs

Le cordonnier, shoemender, will do minor repairs while you wait. Or you could go to *un talon minute*, heel bar, in a store.

Hairdressers and barbers

Both are known as *le salon de coiffure* or *le coiffeur*, and normally open Tuesday to Saturday from 9.30 to 6. Tipping is expected. Women should book an appointment in advance, particularly for *une mise en pli*, a set. *Une coupe* is a cut and *un brushing* a blow-dry.

At large in France — from Sightseeing to Sport

General de Gaulle once wondered how it was possible to govern a country which produces more than 300 cheeses —or words to that effect. He might have said the same about a nation consisting of nearly 37,000 communes. The commune is the oldest administrative unit in France and also the smallest, although it can be anything from a tiny hamlet to a conurbation like Lyon. Its mayor is elected every six years and frequently re-elected for a long term. He is a personage of great standing, as readers of the novel *Clochemerle* or, indeed, of the newspapers, know: Chaban-Delmas of Bordeaux, Defferre of Marseille, Chirac of Paris are all national figures. He also plays a vital part in local affairs (see p. 37). If there is an explanation for the peculiarly provincial feel of French life, it is the strength of the commune as an entity.

By contrast, *le département*, which is the next rung up, has never caught on in terms of emotional attachment. France is divided into 96 *départements*. Apart from the newer ones around Paris, these are all roughly the same size in area, having been designed so that a horse-drawn official could reach any part of his domain from its capital between dawn and dusk. The system was imposed, rather arbitrarily, by the French revolutionaries and reinforced by Napoleon in the person of the *préfets*. The prefect's chief responsibility has always been the maintenance of law and order and control of the police. Thus *la préfecture* is the capital town of a *département*, as well as the headquarters and office of the prefect. In a specialized sense, *la préfecture de police*, means the main Paris police station, located on the Ile de la Cité.

The *départements* are numbered in alphabetical order, from Ain, 01, to Val d'Oise, 95 (Corsica is divided into 2A and 2B). These numbers are used to make up the postal codes. For instance, the code for Nevers in the Nièvre *département*, 58, is 58000. They also complete the registration number of French cars, which is useful if you want to know where other drivers have come

Finding your bearings

La commune

Le département

from, and particularly for avoiding Parisians on the road
— their numbers end in 75, 78, 91 and 95.

Regions   Since 1964 France has also been parcelled out into 22
regions. These more or less coincide with the tourist
map and each has a regional tourist authority. Many of
the regions also correspond to the old provinces of
France. Their names — Provence, Auvergne, Normandie
and so on — are still current usage, as are others —
Anjou, Pays Basque, for example — which legally are no
more than a figment of the imagination.

Changes   It can all be very confusing for the outsider. You have
only to compare two general maps of France: the
names are bound to be different. Even some *département*
names have changed; Basses-Alpes in the south is now
known as Alpes-de-Haute-Provence. Watch out too for
the anglicized spelling used in some guidebooks: Orleans
for Orléans and Lyons for Lyon don't matter much, but
it is irritating to find Rheims instead of the French
Reims, especially when searching through an index.

Exploring   For many people, Paris is the star attraction of France.
Paris   It is organized on unique but simple lines. The capital
is divided into districts called *arrondissements* (each with
its own mayor), which are numbered from 1 to 20 and
spiral out clockwise, starting from the Louvre in the Ier
arrondissement.
  Broadly speaking, the inner circle from the Ier to the
IXe contains most of the places of historical and cultural
interest — the Ile de la Cité, original core of Paris, Ste-
Chapelle and Notre-Dame; the Jardin du Luxembourg,
the Panthéon and the Sorbonne; the Louvre, the Tuileries,
the Jeu de Paume, the Pompidou Centre and the Opéra;
the Champs-Elysées and Arc de Triomphe; the Eiffel
Tower, the Invalides and the Ecole Militaire. Here too
are 'villages' like the Latin Quarter, St-Germain des Prés
and the restored Marais, many museums and galleries,
the famous *boulevards*, shops and department stores,
exclusive restaurants and luxury hotels. And this is the
seat of officialdom, with ministries and government
buildings, embassies, offices and banks.
  The eastern districts, X^e to XIVe and XVIIe to XXe,
are less glamorous. Old streets of workshops, small
factories and shops and shabby dwellings mingle with

tower blocks, new developments and bare construction sites. But there are attractions, notably Montmartre with it highly visible basilica and Bohemian atmosphere, Clichy and Pigalle with day-time markets and night-time cabaret, Montparnasse, now associated chiefly with night life and a hideous new skyscraper, and the Père Lachaise cemetery.

The remaining areas of the west, XVe to XVIIe, tend to be smartly residential, with imposing apartment blocks, expensive boutiques, modern international hotels and once-fashionable Bois de Boulogne on the borders. Parisians talk of the *troisième, quatrième* and so on; someone might say (if they were lucky) that they lived in the *septième*. It's helpful to have some grasp of the system, since restaurants and hotels, museums and galleries are listed by *arrondissement* (or *ardt*, the abbreviation) in the various publications.

Maps and guides

To make the most of Paris, maps and guides are essential. The *Plan de Paris* can be bought at any news stand and contains an excellent map of the city and plan of the public transport system, together with an alphabetical street directory. Pocket maps of the Métro and bus networks can be obtained free at many stations.

Michelin produce a green guide to Paris in English, a town plan (no. 10), index plan (no. 11) and public transport map (no. 9). There is also a supplement to the red guide to hotels and restaurants, and a green guide for the surrounding region of the Ile-de-France. (For road maps, see p. 60.)

Seeing the sights

The best way to get around the centre of Paris is on foot (but see p. 67 for public transport). Like many other capitals, it is surprisingly small and compact, with the main sights clustered along the Seine. Guidebooks suggest suitable itineraries for the pedestrian. These you can follow at your own pace, interspersing culture with café halts, which are expensive in Paris, or shopping or a stroll beside the river.

For the determined tourist, the capital offers highly organized programmes of events − coach tours, boat trips, dinner and cabaret outings, excursions to the Loire valley and so on. You can find out about all these from the main Paris tourist office.

Those of a more independent frame of mind will buy

a copy of *Pariscope* or *L'Officiel des Spectacles*. Each cost a mere two francs or so and lists all the theatres, shows, night clubs, museums and art galleries, plus their opening times. You could supplement these with *Passion*, a more expensive but invaluable guide, in English. It contains helpful information on hospitals, dentists, post offices, banks together with recommendations on restaurants, bars, galleries, parks, bookshops — everything for the English-speaking visitor.

Sightseeing   Tourists of all nationalities converge in their hordes on the châteaux of the Loire valley and Ile-de-France. The *Châteaux*   most famous, such as Chenonceaux, Blois, Azay-le-Rideau and Amboise, Versailles, Chantilly and Fontainebleau, can be unbearably crowded in the summer. To add to the congestion, most of them insist on conducted tours, with pre-programmed guides who speak only French.

There's a lot to be said for skipping the interiors altogether, unless you are well up on the French past and historical significance, as well as the language. The average château has little to offer inside, apart from fine tapestries and perhaps a magnificant staircase, and nothing to compare with the splendour of its external architecture and setting. You will often do better to admire a château from a distance and wander around the grounds.

Son-et-lumière, sound-and-light, is a painless way of imbibing culture. These productions are put on by the great châteaux in the high season, though almost always in French. Concerts, fêtes, horse-races and other events are frequently staged in the big parks as well.

A few days' exploration of the château country will lead you to many lesser residences, virtually undiscovered by the masses. Some are no more than manor houses, but equally fascinating; others may still be lived in and the owners themselves will show you round.

Most châteaux have shorter visiting hours in winter. Smaller ones sometimes close completely between October and April, and many are shut one day a week, probably a Tuesday. Lunchtime closing, from 12 to 2, is common.

Churches   Lovers of ecclesiastical buildings will find something to delight them in just about every corner of France.

Vézelay represents the Romanesque riches of Burgundy, Le Puy the more decorative tradition of the Auvergne, and Chartres, Beauvais, Senlis and Amiens the Gothic grandeur of the north.

There are no special rules about visiting churches, except for those on dress and behaviour dictated by one's own sense of decorum. Admission is free and you can roam at will, though you might have to pay for the tower or crypt.

Churches are often locked between 12 and 2, and you should not go in *pendant les offices*, during services.

Tuesday is the main closing day for museums and galleries, including national ones like the Louvre, Beaubourg Centre and Jeu de Paume in Paris. They generally shut on public holidays as well. Admission is often free (*gratuit*) or half price on Wednesday and Sunday. Normal entrance fees are about 10 to 15f. *Museums and galleries*

However, you can find some places open in Paris on a Tuesday. These are the museums owned by the city, which close on Mondays. They also admit senior citizens free. City of Paris museums include Le Petit Palais, Carnavalet and Balzac's house.

There are the usual reductions for children, students and pensioners at most museums. You might be refused admission half an hour before closing. It's always worth checking opening hours and days in a guidebook.

Museums and galleries are usually quieter between 12 and 2.30 when most French people are busy eating lunch. Sundays can be very crowded.

Garden visiting is not as well publicized in France as in Britain, nor as commercialized. However, Villandry, near Tours, is one of the best known French gardens. It is a modern reconstruction of a sixteenth-century château garden, with vegetables and herbs planted by colour and flanked by box hedges and rose trees. Two more notable gardens in the Loire, but less well-known, are those of the châteaux of Cheverny and Ménars. *Gardens*

The greatest French garden designer, Le Nôtre, has left his mark around Paris, at Versailles, Chantilly and Vaux-le-Vicomte. His style may have been formal, but his coat of arms consisted of three slugs and a spade topped with cabbage leaves. Within the capital, he was responsible for the Jardin des Tuileries (very formal).

Also worth seeing are the celebrated Jardin du Luxembourg, the Jardin des Plantes or botanical gardens, the Parc Monceau for its trees, and the garden of the Musée Rodin for its many varieties of rose.

North-east of Paris, the Parc d'Ermenonville is the earliest example of French landscape gardening. It contains the tomb of Rousseau, though not his body which is in the Panthéon. The Arboretum des Barres is not far from Montargis, south of Fontainebleau, but you need to make an appointment. Further afield, Monet's garden is in the village of Giverny in Normandy. And in the south, many of the Riviera resorts, among them Eze, Menton and Monaco, have wonderful tropical gardens.

Other sights   It's often possible to visit more unusual sights — breweries and nuclear power stations in the north, hydroelectric dams on the Rhone, mineral water plants in Alsace and Lorraine, *fruitières* for cheese manufacture in the Jura, not to mention vineyards in winegrowing areas (see p. 119). Refer to the Michelin green guides or consult the local tourist office.

Sports and distractions   The major form of activity in France seems to be walking or, preferably, driving to the nearest café or restaurant. Yet strangely enough, the French are a very sporting nation, and increasingly so. Sport ranks along with the other indulgences that many people can now afford, such as a car, boat, cottage or holiday. Sailing, skiing, cycling, horseriding and tennis have all surged in popularity. Running has been slower to catch on and the French jogger is a rare sight, although Paris has a marathon in May like other trendy capitals.

From the visitor's point of view, France provides excellent opportunities and facilities for all manner of sports. If you have a particular penchant for water skiing or potholing, refer to the Michelin green guides to find out where these and other *sports et distractions* are on offer.

The Touring Club de France (TCF), apart from assisting drivers on the road, can advise about numerous pursuits, including boating, cycling, horseriding, shooting, fishing and camping. Another good source of information, notably for sailing, canoeing and climbing, is the Union Nationale des Centres Sportifs de Plein Air. (See p. 167 for useful addresses.)

Reproduced by courtesy of the artist

For cycling and walking, see pp. 71 and 76.

You can always find somewhere to swim in France. *Swimming*
Nearly every town has *sa piscine municipale*, swimming
pool, and proudly proclaims the fact if it's *chauffée*,
heated. These are usually pleasant, well-run and under
patronized. It's often compulsory to wear a cap, but you
can usually hire one. In the countryside, quiet rivers,
neglected canals and hidden lakes abound, with anglers
as the sole competition. Such rustic waters are generally
clean and safe enough for a dip, but you should avoid
any that flow through urban areas. The Seine, Gironde
and Garonne are particularly dirty. In the Jura, a few of
the lakes are too dangerous for bathers. Lac Léman

(Lake Geneva) and the others in the Alps are now largely free of pollution, although they can be very cold.

For swimming in the sea, you have the choice of the bracing Channel and Atlantic or the Mediterranean. The latter has the worst record for pollution, especially bad between Menton and St-Raphael and near Marseille; and the east coast of Corsica suffers from the products of Italian chemical plants. But it doesn't follow that the rest of the French coastline is pure: La Rochelle, Trouville and Cherbourg are among the black spots.

The beach or *la plage* is free almost everywhere. However, in the Mediterranean it's worth paying to get on to a private bit, away from the crowds and dirt of the public beach. Most resorts are discreetly supervised by lifeguards, who sometimes operate a flag system to show when swimming is safe. It can be quite dangerous on the Atlantic coast. *Baignade interdite* means no bathing. There is often a play area where you can leave your children, for a fee. It may be called le Mickey Club. Beach umbrellas and deckchairs can normally be hired.

Toplessness has become almost universal, but those sensitive to local feeling will check before baring their breasts. Total nudism is officially confined to the *camps de nudistes*, nudist camps, which are flourishing, particularly on the Languedoc coast. However, nakedness sometimes encroaches on ordinary beaches.

The *Guide des Plages*, obtainable from many French bookstalls, gives information on beaches and their facilities and a pollution report for the entire coast. Inland bathing places and swimming pools are indicated on the Michelin yellow maps.

Fishing   *La pêche*, fishing, is practised by about one-fifth of the population. There are countless rivers and lakes to choose from, most of them productive of pike, perch, black bass, roach and bream. Some of the best trout fishing is in the Jura, but trout, salmon and their relatives char and grayling can be found in other mountainous areas, as well as the Auvergne, Brittany and elsewhere.

Rivers are classified into *première catégorie*, described as *salmonidés dominants*, that is trout streams; and *deuxième catégorie, salmonidés non dominants*, where maggots may be used as bait. The season varies according to region, but typically it might be 1 March to 15 September for the first category, and 15 January to 15

April for the second. You can start fishing half an hour
before dawn and must stop half an hour after sunset.
There are national regulations governing the minimum
permitted size of fish caught or *longeur minimum des
prises*.

On private land, where it will probably say *pêche
réservée*, private fishing, you have to get the owner's
permission. On public land — canals, navigable rivers,
large lakes — fishing rights belong to the state. In both
cases, you need a licence.

Start at the tourist office, who will probably direct
you to the nearest tackle shop or even a café to acquire
un permis. The rules change from one *département* to
the next and you should consult the office of Eaux et
Forêts for further information, or the local Association
de Pêche et de Pisciculture. If you want to do serious fly
fishing, you might have to join.

Fishing tackles is *attirail de pêche*. Maggots are
asticots. The Michelin camping guide tells you which
sites have fishing nearby.

Shooting

The French regard *la chasse*, hunting but really shooting,
as a natural right, which of course it once was for many
peasants and those who lived off the land. But the game
have proved unequal to annual massacre by something
like two million highly organized and mobilized gunmen.
This normally occurs in the middle of September, when
everything in sight is shot. It explains the eery stillness
of the forests in France.

Such is the general scarcity of wildlife that the law
has become much more stringent and it is unlikely that
you will participate in a shoot. In theory a visitor is
entitled to two 48-hour *licences de chasse*, shooting
permits, per annum. This involves complex documenta-
tion, including a police testimonial to the effect that you
have never been convicted of a criminal offence. A full
permis de chasse, shooting licence, is almost impossible
to obtain.

Spectator sports

The French are also great spectators. Motor racing or
l'automobilisme arouses much enthusiasm, likewise the
turf, with the famous Paris racecourses of Longchamp
and Chantilly and many more throughout the country.

Le football is followed nationwide and played by well
over a million amateurs. *Le rugby* is particularly strong

in the south, where every town and village has a local
team. Béziers alone supports three clubs. It is mostly
le rugby à quinze, the union game, but *le jeu à treize*,
with 13 a side, is popular in the Midi. Welshmen and
New Zealanders might dispute the French interpreta-
tion of the rules.

The biggest spectacle of all is the Tour de France. The
world's top cycle race grips the whole of France for
three weeks preceding Le Quatorze Juillet or Bastille
Day (14 July). If you happen to be there at the time,
it's inescapable, with blanket coverage in the media and
everyone passionately interested. Villages strive for the
honour of being on the route and donate prizes along
the way; men push cars into ditches to clear a passage
for the race; and families throng the roads, waiting with
their picnics to cheer the riders on. The rules of the race
are intricate and liable to change at any time. But since
they always include a booby prize for the slowest rider,
perhaps it doesn't matter much.

Betting and   Betting is officially controlled in France and its most
gambling   popular expression is *le tiercé*, where huge amounts can
be won by placing the first three horses in a race in the
correct order; there is a smaller prize for the right horses
but wrong order. This is run by the PMU (Pari Mutuel
Urbain), the equivalent of a tote, with branches at
cafés all over France. Sunday morning is the time when
everyone queues to put their bets on the race of the
afternoon.

The *loterie nationale*, national lottery, also sells
thousands of tickets each week, and has its name on
coloured china ashtrays in cafés.

Boules   Men playing *boules* outside the café is a familiar and
uniquely French scene. Although it is particularly
associated with the south, the game actually originated
in Lyon. An annual tournament is held here in the place
Bellecour at Whitsun.

It's a sort of French version of bowls. Matches are
between teams of three, *triplettes*, or four, *quadrettes*,
using iron-clad balls. The object of the attacking team is
to throw the balls as close as possible to a small ball at
the end of the pitch; the defending team must dislodge
the opponents' balls and supplant them, which the
skilled are able to achieve very accurately. When played

without moving the feet, it is called *à la pétanque*, which is the Provençal variant and the name of the game in the south; with three steps, it is known as *à la longue*.

La pelote is the national sport of the Basques. Basically, it is played between two teams who alternately hit the ball against a high wall, either with the hand, bare or gloved, or with a wooden board, or with a special curved piece of willow. The ball itself is called *la pelote* and, for the proper consistency, should be covered with dog hide.

Pelota

Homemade farces, gangster films and Hollywood extravaganza are the staple fare of the French cinema. American films are widely shown, both in the capital and the provinces, but are invariably dubbed. However, look out for the letters *VO* in cities, which means that the film will be in the original language (*version originale*).

Cinema

Paris is a mecca for the serious film enthusiast, with the emphasis on quality films from all over the world. Apart from the expensive luxury cinemas of the Champs-Elysées, there are hundreds of smaller houses throughout the capital.

The most surprising thing about a French cinema is that you must tip the usherette. One franc is acceptable. Some films are banned to those under 18, others to those under 13. It will simply say this at the cinema — *interdit aux moins de 13/18 ans*. If your youthful appearance could arouse suspicion, take a document with proof of age. Pornography is a fringe interest, now confined to designated cinemas.

Performances are usually continuous until 1 a.m. Smoking is not allowed. Students can buy reduced-price tickets.

Plays, concerts and other performances normally start at 9 in the evening, occasionally 8.30. Most theatres close one day a week. Tickets can be reserved in advance through the theatre or concert hall or an agency. Usherettes and cloakroom attendants expect a tip.

Theatre, music, ballet

Communicating

The spoken word accompanies every encounter in France, or certainly in the provinces. In shops, restaurants, service stations, wherever you go, you will be greeted and dismissed with *Bonjour* and *Au revoir, m'sieurs-dames*, said very fast, regardless of your sex and number.

Paris is a different picture. Its citizens are in too much of a hurry to bother and they have never been noted for their warmth. French people can indeed be brusque and foreigners should be prepared for this. But the general impression, especially in the country, is one of politeness, which the visitor can at least reciprocate.

Even those with rudimentary French, or none, should prepare themselves to give and return the everyday salutations. These are *bonjour* for good morning and good afternoon; *bonsoir* for good evening, from about 6 onwards, and good night; *au revoir* for goodbye. *Bonsoir* is said on both arriving and leaving, whereas *bonne nuit* implies good night, sleep tight; you might be wished *bonsoir et bonne nuit* when you go to bed in a hotel. *A tout à l'heure* is a much used expression, equivalent to see you later or 'bye for now. Probably the best response is *Oui, à tout à l'heure*, or just *Oui*, yes. Use *Monsieur, Madame* or *Mademoiselle* with every greeting.

So much the better if you can extend to *Ça va?*, more formally *Comment allez-vous?*, how are you, to which the answer is *Très bien, merci, et vous?*, very well thank you, and you?. The same reply will serve for *Vous avez bien dormi?*, did you sleep well, an inquiry French people tend to make until about noon when you're staying with them.

S'il vous plaît, abbreviated to *s.v.p.* on signs, means please. *Merci* is thank you, but also means *no* thank you; *merci beaucoup/bien* is thank you very much. *Pardon* is the best word to use if you want to stop someone in the street and ask the way. It also means sorry, excuse me, as does *excusez-moi*. *Je voudrais*, I would like, sounds less rude than I want (*je veux*).

You don't need to invert the sentence to pose a question. Just express it as a statement and raise your voice at the end, for instance, *C'est un poisson?*, is it a fish?.

It's useful to know how to pronounce the alphabet in French, or at least the letters of your name. Double-barrelled names cause mystification, so if you have one it's easier to shorten it for daily dealings.

Some foreigners have the knack of communicating in French with only a hazy idea of the grammar and a small vocabulary. They are usually extroverts and good mimics. The secret is to concentrate on intonation and rhythm, rather than worrying about tenses and constructions, and to deliver the words with aplomb. A Gallic shrug might achieve more than searching for the correct word. For maximum effect, you should look as if you're speaking the language, though it may feel exaggerated to you. Watch the French and you will see how strenuous it is: each syllable is stressed and faces are contorted by pronunciation, lips protruding in a round O or drawn back in a slit. Gesticulations add further emphasis.

Your efforts to converse in French will generally be appreciated. And the chances of mutual understanding at any level are improved, now that the French have begun to bow to the inevitable and acknowledge the world supremacy of the English language over their own. English has become the first choice as a foreign language in schools and universities. So you're less likely to meet a blank stare and pretended ignorance.

Idiomatic French

You will notice that letters and words are often dropped in spoken French — *j'suis* for *je suis, on peut pas* for *on ne peut pas, faut pas* for *il ne faut pas*. It can aid comprehension when you realise this.

It's fine to respond in kind to a hi or hello with *salut*, but you should tread carefully where colloquialism is concerned. Slang has a limited life in any language and it can sound ridiculous in the mouth of a foreigner; just imagine a Frenchwoman describing something as ripping or neat.

Nevertheless, there are some expressions which it is helpful to understand, if not employ. *Sympa*, short for *sympathique*, is the French equivalent of nice. *Vachement* is an emphatic very or really, verging on the risky (e.g. *vachement bon*, bloody good). *Un type vachement sympa* would be a really good/nice guy/bloke. *D'accord* or *oké* is OK.

Le machin or *le truc* have already been mentioned (see p. 51). They can refer to any object whose name you don't know and are particularly useful in plumbing and motoring situations.

Ficher is an all-purpose verb and less offensive than *foutre* (vulgarly, to do, give etc.) — *je m'en fiche*, I don't care/mind (*ça m'est égal*); *il ne fiche rien*, he isn't doing a thing (*il ne fait rien*). *Fiche-moi le camp* is clear off, beat it, but in dire straits *fous-moi le camp* should have real impact, or *foutez-moi le camp* if you're being pestered by more than one.

Local language

To the visitor, the most striking thing about French as it is spoken in the south and south-west is the sing-song intonation. The last syllable of a word, which is normally silent, is often pronounced and even stressed; thus Provence becomes 'Provence-uh'. There is a nasal quality too: *vin* (wine) sounds like the English 'vain' and *cent*, confusingly, can come out like *cinq* (5 instead of 100). People tend to say *eh bé* for *eh bien* (well), and *té pardi* instead of *bien sûr* (of course).

You're not likely to encounter a speaker of pure Occitan, unless it's a trendy intellectual. This is the ancient *langue d'oc*, the original tongue of southern France, and is closer to Italian and Spanish than French. Some examples of the vocabularly are *aiga* for *eau* (water); *galina* for *poule* (hen); *oustal* for *maison* (house); *frech* for *froid* (cold). There are 24 tenses, apparently. However, many locals speak 'Francitan' — French with a sprinkling of Occitan.

On the Atlantic coast, people have a slow measured speech which accentuates the rolling of the Rs. The Basques, of course, are distinguished by a separate language, known as the Escuara, while at the eastern end of the Pyrenees, in the Roussillon, Catalan is spoken as well as French. Corsicans too have their own language, with a strong Italian influence, but it is largely confined to speech and rarely written down.

The Touraine is still considered to be the region where the purist French can be heard, and its natives pride themselves on the fact when away from home. In Brittany, people can remember when it was a punishable offence to speak Breton. This is no longer the case and the language is actively fostered in schools and the media, though less than half the population use it. Even in Alsace, which was the most sensitive spot linguistically, French is now the main language. However, the dialects, of which there are several, can be found here. The chief one is basically high German plus a smattering of French words, all delivered with a noticeable lilt.

In the 1960s trendy French people, especially those in advertising and the *media*, began to refer to *le shopping* and *le standing*. Anglo-Saxon words invaded the language, causing such alarm to purists that a law was passed in 1977 banning the use of foreign words in public when there was a French alternative. Where possible intruders were repelled by French words; for instance, *bouteur* officially replaced *bulldozer*, though it never caught on.

Franglais

The *franglais* fashion and the sense of outrage it provoked are over. But there are many survivors like *le parking* and *le weekend* which are now permanent fixtures. In fact, several had been borrowed earlier and only came under attack at the height of the *franglais* craze. Others, such as *le club* and *le bifteck*, have been established since the eighteenth century. And words like *l'environnement*, with a respectable Latin root, have gained new meaning. Even the Robert French dictionary is defeated by *sexy*, which it defines as *qui a du sex-appeal* (one who has sex appeal).

Radio France, the state radio, is divided into three networks. France-Inter broadcasts news bulletins and magazine programmes, with light music and the occasional play. During the summer holiday season, it gives the news, weather and road conditions in English twice a day, at 9 a.m. and 4 p.m. France-Musique is devoted to serious music, mainly classical but also contemporary and jazz. France-Culture concentrates on highbrow talks, interviews and debates.

Radio and television

Most French people in fact tune in to foreign stations like Europe One, Radio Télé-Luxembourg and Radio Monte-Carlo. In general, they still prefer listening to the radio to watching television, and it's not hard to understand why. French television, compared to British at any rate, is humdrum.

At present, there are three TV channels — again a

state monopoly, and financed by advertising and annual licence fees. These are Télévision Française 1 (TF1), Antenne 2 (A2) and France Régions 3 (FR3).

The written word

Written French is a different animal from the popular French that everyone speaks. Dense with meaning yet supposedly lucid, it used to be the language of international diplomacy. Now it is a literary form, full of long words of Latin descent and classical constructions, and uttered only by deluded foreign students.

While most of the French themselves find the novels of Proust and Balzac heavy going, the language has been taken to extremes of obfuscation at the pens of intellectuals like Barthes and the structuralists. Nor is the newspaper *Le Monde* exactly light reading, with its insistence on the almost defunct past historic tense instead of the ordinary perfect (*il arriva* for *il est arrivé*).

Letter-writing

The French do not just dash off impulsive notes to each other. Writing is a serious matter and governed by strict rules.

Business letters are the height of pomposity. They open with *Monsieur* or *Madame* or *Monsieur le Directeur* and proceed with a great deal of mannered verbiage and roundabout ways of saying yes or no, before ending with a long-winded flourish. The French have kept a whole gamut of respectful phrases, each one subtly different in degree. Everything hinges on the circumstances, the relationship of the sender to the recipient, whether it is a man addressing a woman and so forth. If you want to be absolutely certain of correctness, you should consult a book of etiquette as the French do.

For most purposes, however, an acceptable formula for Yours faithfully, to someone you don't know, or know very slightly, is *Veuillez agréer, Monsieur/Madame, mes sentiments distingués* (kindly accept, Sir/Madam, my distinguished sentiments). This would do for a letter to a hotelier reserving a room. To a superior you would have to raise the tone to *Veuillez agréer, Monsieur le Directeur, l'expression de mes sentiments respectueux et dévoués* (kindly accept, Mr Director Sir, the expression of my respectful and devoted sentiments). The *Monsieur* or *Madame* must always be spelt out.

To someone you already know quite well you could start *Cher Monsieur/Chère Madame* and finish with

Veuillez croire, cher Monsieur/chère Madame, à mes meilleurs sentiments (kindly believe, dear Sir/Madam, in my better feelings). This might be suitable for a polite thank-you letter: it is not going over the top to express a thousand thanks or *mille remerciements*.

Only where you are convinced of being on fairly intimate terms could you open with *Cher ami/Chère amie* (dear friend) or *Mon cher X/Ma chère X* (my dear X, but never *Mon cher ami*, my dear friend, which implies condescension), and round off with *Bien amicalement à vous/toi* (in a very friendly way to you) or *Amitiès* (friendships), or for someone dear *Je t'embrasse bien affectueusement* (I kiss you very affectionately).

The French like to make their written communications even more formal by using plain white cards. On these are sent congratulations or condolences, replies to invitations, and New Year greetings (rather than Christmas cards, which they don't really go in for).

The date

Writing the date, at least, is straightforward. It is put at the top of a letter as le 19 septembre 1983 or le 3 mai 1984, no capitals and no -ths and -nds except for the first of the month, as le 1er juillet 1985.

Handwriting and figures

French handwriting is distinctive and always the same, presumably as a result of the education system, with fat letters, loops and twirls.

Handwritten numbers can be a bit bewildering. Look out for ꟾ = 1, ꟻ = 5, ꟼ = 7, ꟿ = 9. 1st, 2nd and 3rd appear as 1er or 1ère (*premier/première*), 2e (*deuxième*) 3e (*troisième*) and so on.

The French use a comma instead of a decimal point. Thus 0.5 is 0,5 and this applies to the way prices are written (see p. 24).

Conversely, they express thousands with a point or a gap where we would place a comma, making 25,000 into 25.000 or 25 000.

Books

French books always have the contents or *table des matières* at the back, not the front. They are often rather tatty-looking, with thick paper, rough and sometimes uncut edges, and bound in brown wrapping paper.

Newspapers and magazines

A national press as such scarcely exists in France and provincial papers account for most of the total sales of daily newspapers. *Ouest-France*, published in Rennes, has the highest circulation in the country.

The provincial papers do, of course, deal with national news, but in a routine way. They are bulked out with page after page of local items and, for even more parochial coverage, many are printed in multiple editions. However, they can be useful for finding about accommodation, village fêtes and the weather.

Of the Parisian dailies, *Le Monde* is probably the best known, and has the widest circulation abroad. It is issued in the afternoon with the next day's date, which means that Wednesday's paper is really Tuesday's. *Le Figaro* is its rival among the heavies. *L'Humanité* is the Communist newspaper. *Libération* is the 'in' newspaper.

Newspapers are rarely delivered. Instead French people might buy one most days at the tobacconists or news-stand, and will very probably subscribe to a weekly, such as *L'Express* or *Le Nouvel Observateur*.

French journalists are not very good at distinguishing news from comment. And, in the cause of stylistic elegance, they go to ludicrous lengths to avoid repeating a name: you need your wits about you to remember that M. Jean X is also *le deputé de Y* and *le secrétaire général de Z*, and will be referred to as such in subsequent paragraphs. Even the business pages talk of *le billet vert*, the green note, instead of *le dollar*. Mrs Thatcher is inevitably *la dame de fer*, the iron lady.

The president is often called l'Elysée (the name of his residence). Le Quai d'Orsay means the foreign office, and l'Hôtel Matignon the prime minister's, on the same principle. Abbreviations can be impenetrable until you realize that most of them are back to front, like OTAN for NATO and OLP for the PLO. Others are more obscure, such as *PNB* for GNP (gross national product). *DOM* stands for an overseas *département* (like Guadeloupe), *HLM* for council housing, *SMIC* for the legal minimum wage.

The weather forecast or *la méteo* is usually presented as a map of France with symbols and regional predictions. Key words are *la pluie*, rain; *le brouillard*, fog; *le verglas*, ice; *la neige*, snow; *les averses*, showers; *le vent fort*, strong wind; *brumeux*, misty; *nuageux*, cloudy; *les ondées orageuses*, heavy showers; *les éclaircies*, sunny intervals.

Dealing with the French

Social relations are still very formal in France. Christian names are not bandied about in the American style, nor is it unheard-of for women friends to address each other as *Madame*. Much store is set by titles like *Monsieur le Président*, although the particular gentleman may have long since retired as a company chairman. A few elderly married couples even continue to use the respectful *vous* to each other. In most families, however, the intimate *tu* is standard, as it is among students and, increasingly, among the younger generation altogether.

But, as a visitor, you should always say *vous*, unless there are definite indications that you can be more familiar. The only categories where *tutoiement* is safe from the start are children and dogs, although you must use *vous* to the cat. Similarly, you should err on the side of caution and call everyone *monsieur, madame* or *mademoiselle*, until invited to do otherwise.

Everyday manners

The kissing of a woman's hand by a man is virtually obsolete in France, except as an exaggerated display of gallantry. But the French shake hands at every opportunity. Strangely enough this habit, often thought to be typically English, is now much more common in France. However, *le shake-hand* did originate in England and was brought over the Channel by dandified gentlemen in the early nineteenth century.

In France you shake hands when meeting someone and parting from them, on being introduced and at subsequent encounters. This includes when saying goodnight, if you're staying with people. An inferior is always presented to a superior, that is a younger person to an older one, a man to a woman. The handshake is practised between schoolchildren from the age of about 12, and between whole families, which can be a lengthy process if they are Catholic. It is the most usual form of greeting from one man to another. Men also shake hands with women, although the woman should offer her hand first, and women with women. But after two or

Shaking hands and kissing

three reunions new conventions arise and you have to gauge whether to advance to the next level.

This is kissing, which is a normal salutation too. Again, it was an old English custom, widespread in Tudor times and the object of astonishment to travellers from the Continent, like Erasmus who delighted in it.

Kissing takes place between relatives, obviously, and between acquaintances who have reached more familiar terms without necessarily being intimate friends. Men very rarely kiss each other, despite popular notions about the Latin temperament, but close chums might hug each other and fathers don't seem to be shy about embracing their grown-up sons.

Both handshaking and kissing are important to the French as marks of physical recognition. It is impolite not to give one or the other, even if you bump into someone in the street, and foreigners should be prepared for this. On the other hand, you are not expected to demonstrate great exuberance in the performance. The French handshake is a fairly limp-wristed affair, not an energetic, manly grip; and the kiss always consists of two light pecks, one on each cheek, delivered high up and well away from the mouth.

Most visitors will probably be confined to shaking hands. In any case, you should follow the lead of your French hosts or friends. Beware, incidentally, of the word *baiser*, which has a more vulgar meaning than the innocent to kiss (*embrasser* is safer).

At home with the French

The chances of your being at home with the French, still less feeling it, are slim. The French are not so much inhospitable as different. One word for the home is *le foyer*, the hearth, but also the household and by extension the family itself — that all-important feature of French life. The home is the inner sanctum and any outsider who is admitted must show proper respect for it and recognize the honour of the occasion.

In practice, this means that the French prefer to have a jolly time with friends in a café or restaurant, and to reserve the home for formal entertaining. The latter, at its most extreme, takes the shape of *la réception*, with all the trappings of a bygone age, or at least some of them — printed invitations, evening dress, hired waiters, the finest silver and glass.

The guests duly arrived, the hostess leads the way to

the table and positions herself at one end, the host at the other, with the most exalted guests on their right hands. When they have sat down, perhaps after grace, everyone else follows suit. Each place is set with a battery of implements — soup spoon, fish knife and fork, table knife and fork, and possibly an oyster fork or snail extractor; the principle is to work in from the outside. The range of glasses includes a large one for water, a smaller one for red wine, a smaller still for white wine, and a tall *flûte* for Champagne. The napkin, which matches the tablecloth, may conceal a bread roll. Starting with the most eminent guests, the dishes are presented from the left. Everything comes round again, apart from the salad, cheese and fruit, so you have to leave room for a second helping and at the same time ensure that you finish all the food on your plate. It is polite to comment on its quality. Plates are whisked away after each course and new cutlery distributed after the fish. The final act of the performance occurs in the drawing room or *le salon*, where everybody withdraws for coffee, always black, and a liqueur or *un pousse-café*. No one will depart before the most important guest.

This is the kind of theatre which is still put on among the most select circles of society in Paris. No wonder Parisians have such a formidable reputation. But there is a lot of truth in their image, sometimes wrongly foisted on the French as a whole, as stand-offish, intolerant, aggressive, if not positively hostile; and it endears them neither to foreigners nor to fellow Frenchmen. Parisians seldom issue invitations, partly because they have to do things perfectly, partly because they may be ashamed of their own cramped apartments. When they do, it is to their exclusive set, without any attempt to introduce new blood.

In the country, in their second homes, Parisians might be more forthcoming, but only to their own kind. If you happen to be staying with them, they go to tremendous lengths to please. Delicious meals are prepared, the best wines brought up from the cellar, excursions planned for sightseeing and shopping. They even ask friends round, but not, it often turns out, to meet you the honoured guest, simply to talk among themselves.

Nevertheless, there has been a general easing of starchiness, both in the capital and in the provinces. When an invitation is extended, it's more likely to be

Venez dîner à la fortune du pot or, simpler, *Venez manger, ce sera à la bonne franquette* or, for a drink, *Venez prendre un verre à la maison* (come and eat, take pot luck, or come and have a drink at the house). But you must still be invited, if only verbally: the person who drops in unannounced will be cordially received, but rarely offered a coffee or drink.

You can probably judge for yourself what degree of casualness is really implied. To err on the safe side, you should arrive punctually and instruct any offspring to be on their best behaviour. The French home is one place where other people's children are expected to be unobtrusive.

A drink with your landlord or the local farmer might sound innocent, but can turn out to be quite an ordeal. You will probably be sat round a table as the host dispenses his homemade wine, a sweet sherry-type brew of great potency. There is no choice. Glasses will be clinked with a *Santé*, cheers, or *A la vôtre*, your health, and refilled with alacrity. In front of you are bowls of peanuts and crisps specially bought for the evening, which must be consumed eagerly, not toyed with. There is no questioning the hospitality. And the further you are from Paris, the greater it is.

In a small village, the French can demonstrate their friendliness. If you're renting a holiday home, you may be regarded as a being from outer space, but that's probably all the more reason to shower you with gifts. The chances are that neighbours will call, sooner or later, bearing melons or grapes or beans or fish (probably live), or whatever is in season. The generosity can be overwhelming, even though it is also a means of getting rid of surplus produce.

Thanks   How do you reciprocate? If your holiday is short, there's little you can do except satisfy their curiosity about yourself and invite them in for a drink. However, if you go back to the same place year after year, you'll know what to expect and can come armed with suitable presents. Whisky always goes down well; but any speciality of your native land, even if it seems trite to you, will be appreciated.

The same sort of forward planning is useful when staying with a French family: your gift has an extra cachet if it's not easily obtainable in France. Tea has a certain snob value, as do British goods like Stilton cheese, smoked salmon, Christmas pudding, shortbread.

If you're invited round to someone's house, it's quite all right to bring flowers with you or a bottle of wine, just as you might do anywhere else. For a really formal occasion, however, it is customary to arrive empty-handed and then send a note of thanks to the hostess afterwards. This should be accompanied by flowers, fruit or chocolates. To be absolutely correct, the flowers should all be the same variety. Don't choose chrysanthemums, which are associated with death. Red roses are doubly taboo, since they express intimate affection and are now identified with the socialist party, which could be a serious indiscretion.

The French and their reputation

Even before you arrive in France, you will probably have various notions of what French people are really like. They have had a bad press, and this makes them notorious for arrogance, brusqueness and inhospitality among other things. Unfortunately, you might well come across these characteristics.

The French, it must be admitted, are not always easy to like. They have neither the sunny open disposition of southern Europeans, nor the stolid but obvious reserve of northerners. Although this book has conveyed a generally favourable impression of the French (based on personal experience), it's only fair to warn you of the worst you can expect. Parts of this section take the bleakest possible view; others seek to explain what makes French people tick (an impossible undertaking).

National stereotypes are always misleading, and this is particularly the case with France, whose inhabitants think of themselves as Norman, Burgundian, Auvergnat first and foremost and as French second. So the kind of reception you will get depends very much on where you are. At risk of generalization again, residents of the south and west tend to be more open and friendly than those of the north and east. And there is certainly a contrast between city dwellers and country folk all over France, with the latter more inclined to be welcoming.

Don't whatever you do, imagine that Parisians are representative of French people as a whole. They are exceptional, in the same way as New Yorkers or Londoners are untypical of their countries, and just as

Reproduced by courtesy of the artist

unpopular in the rest of France as they are in the eyes of foreigners.

It is no accident that *étranger*, the French for foreigner, also means stranger and outsider. To French people, everyone outside the family and immediate circle of close friends is a stranger, to be approached with suspicion, and this applies equally to fellow French and to foreigners. So, although they can appear quite forthcoming, willing to pass the time of day or chat to someone in a café, deep down they are reserved and wary, guarding their anonymity.

Consequently, the French do not enter friendship lightly. They make true friends in their youth and stick by them, but they are hopeless at casual mateyness or cultivating a wide range of acquaintances. Professional colleagues remain precisely that and, even after working together for years, rarely make any attempt to meet socially.

The rigid hierarchies of public life are a further disincentive to mixing work with pleasure. Many schools, for example, have separate dining rooms for different grades of teacher. On top of this, there is an in-built reverence for authority, which widens the gap between 'superiors' and 'inferiors', as well as curbing any delegation of responsibility.

All this helps to account for the perversity of French officials, most faceless of bureaucrats. At their hands, you will experience the ultimate in bored indifference. Even a straightforward request for information, such as the time of a train, can turn into an ordeal and leave you wondering whether to trust your informant. But you soon discover that bureaucracy in France exists largely to serve its own purposes, and that these include endless form-filling. The French accept it because they are used to the state legislating on the tiniest details of their private lives, and have been since the Code Napoléon of 1804.

They relish the legal niceties. One of the most absurd laws in France, introduced in 1881, allows the government and property-owners to plaster walls with notices stating that it is forbidden to put up notices on walls — *défense d'afficher*. Drainpipes were overlooked and have, as a result, become the target of posters. This is a classic illustration not only of French logic but also of *le système D* which, thankfully, operates alongside the red tape. The D stands for *débrouille*, meaning resourcefulness. It is simply the art of getting round the system, a time-honoured alternative.

Why do the French have such a bad image? It's an impossible question to answer, but there are clues. For instance, French people, compared to other Europeans, have the most jaundiced view of mankind. Only 5 per cent of them, according to a survey, believed that people are intrinsically good, while 34 per cent of the Irish (who were the most optimistic) took this view. At the same time it was found that the French (with the

Belgians) suffered least from remorse over past misdeeds.

In another survey, nine out of ten French people claimed to be happy. Significantly, they listed the family and health as prime ingredients in their state of bliss. Half of them also mentioned God as a factor. This will come as no surprise to visitors, who see the evidence of religious faith everywhere in France. There's always a sign at the entrance to a town or village giving the times of church services or *heures des messes*.

In fact, the French are much less devout than the Americans as far as regularly attending church goes. Parisians are particuarly heathen, though Bretons remain fervently Catholic and many still wear full mourning when the occasion warrants. But most French people are baptized and married in church, and religion, even if it is superficial, is an important thread in their lives. Church festivals and saints' days dictate their holidays, and family celebrations revolve around christenings, first communions and weddings.

Pets and the The French attitude to animals is a bizarre mix of
French brutality, indifference and adoration. They think nothing of shooting larks and thrushes or keeping live rabbits horribly cooped up at the market; fishermen often cook their catch without killing it first. Where food is concerned, the French simply accept the raw facts — and tend to portray them graphically in cookbook illustrations. In fact, they are altogether unsqueamish, not to say ghoulish, as you will notice if you have the misfortune to come across a road accident.

Yet the French have suddenly become a nation of pet lovers. Between them they own something like 8 million dogs, 6 million cats and 6 million birds. Supermarkets now have whole sections devoted to pet foods, including special 'healthful' ones.

Dogs in particular elicit the same sort of emotions as babies. If you take a puppy for a walk, it will be cooed over and patted by every passer-by, in a way most untypical of the normally reserved behaviour of the French citizen. Dogs are even brought into restaurants and, if small enough, placed on the seat next to the indulgent owner.

However, this does not prevent people abandoning their pets in large numbers when they become inconvenient, at the start of the summer holiday. Stray dogs are common, partly for this reason, partly because the French are inclined to let their dogs wander at will. And no one seems to protest if you hit your own dog. Beware of fouled pavements.

Chauvinism is a French word, coined to describe that **French *v.*** brand of haughty and exclusive patriotism for which the **foreigners** French have long been renowned and which General de Gaulle seemed to embody. (Chauvin was the name of a character representing the fanatical but ignorant Napoleonic soldier.)

The French are convinced of their own rightness. For them, French nationalism has carried a special seal of approval ever since it became synonymous with the message of liberty, equality and fraternity, which may partly explain why it has often collided with the equivalent American belief. The United States was the great bugbear of French foreign policy in the 1960s, and this rubbed off on American tourists, who were assured of a hostile reception in France.

However, Americanization had already begun, even then. American business methods were being copied, with the establishment of schools for budding executives, like Fontainebleau, and the import of terms such as *le public-relations*; *le management* was given the OK and Frenchified pronunciation by the Académie française. American music, films and TV programmes followed, magazines like *L'Express* adopted the American-style format and looked like *Newsweek*, *drugstores* and *snacks* proliferated, and these and other words passed into the language.

The French have finally admitted to a sneaking admiration for American civilization, or many of its facets, which makes them the more inclined to welcome American visitors. Unfortunately, Americans tend to feel little in common with the French, partly because so few know the language. Even the food is a barrier: ordering a Coke or a coffee in the middle of your *rôti de veau* (veal roast) is not the way to a Frenchman's heart.

Relations between France and Britain, or Angleterre as the French insist on calling it, have always been complex. Although contacts have grown closer, with a steady traffic of tourists both ways across the Channel, the centuries-old antagonism has not disappeared. It erupts, periodically, in lamb and apple wars.

The British visit France more than any other country, and like it, as a country. Yet most dislike the French, as people. This gut reaction goes deep and is still bound up with the traditional image of the 'Frogs' living off an inedible diet of garlic, snails and frogs' legs (or whole frogs, as some believe). Frenchness is also associated with naughtiness — French knickers, French letters (rubbers, which are known as *les capotes anglaises* in French), and the Folies Bergères. To this must be added the more realistic attractions of cheap booze and well-stocked shops, which bring daytrippers flocking over to the Channel ports in the cause of international misunderstanding.

Reproduced by courtesy of *Punch*

On the French side too, misconceptions about the British linger, along the lines of bowler hats, queues, constant rain, mint sauce and steamed puddings. At the same time, many British products are considered *snob* — they have stolen the word as well — such as tea, whisky, pop music, Shetland sweaters and kilts. The British monarchy, particularly such aspects of it as Charles and Di (known as 'lay-dee-dee') and the corgis, evokes passionate interest. Incidentally, a mention of Scottish or Irish ancestry always goes down well with French people.

There's no doubt that the French are more receptive to outside influences and to foreign visitors than they used to be. They like going abroad themselves now, which is one sign of a less insular attitude. Hence the unpopularity of President Mitterand's currency restrictions, which were seen as an attempt to curb their globetrotting and lasted less than a year.

Of course, lack of comprehension persists, as it always will do between nations. But it only adds to the mystery of an already enchanted land. If you've never been to France, you will be converted; if you're an old hand, you'll already find it difficult to keep away. *Bon voyage!*

Some Useful Addresses

French Government Tourist Offices abroad	610 Fifth Avenue, New York 10020. 372 Bay Street, Toronto. 178 Piccadilly, London W1V 0AL. 12 Castlereagh Street, Sydney. Government Life Building, Wellington.

Embassies   US: 2 avenue Gabriel, Paris VIIIe; 296—12—02.
UK: 35 rue du faubourg St-Honoré, Paris VIIIe;
     266—91—42.
Australia: 4 rue Jean Rey, Paris XVe; 575—62—00.
Canada: 35 avenue Montaigne, Paris VIIIe; 225—99—55.
New Zealand: 7 ter rue Léonard-de-Vinci, Paris XVIe;
     500—24—11.
South Africa: 59 quai d'Orsay, Paris VIIe; 555—92—37.

Paris   Office de tourisme de Paris,
     127 avenue des Champs-Elysées 75008.
Main post office, 52 rue du Louvre 75100; 233—71—60.
Régie Autonome des Transports Parisiens (RATP),
     place de la Madeleine, VIIIe; tourist office,
     53 bis quai des Grands-Augustins, VIe.
American Express, 11 rue Scribe, IXe; 260—09—99.
Thomas Cook, 2 place de la Madeleine, VIIIe;
     260—33—20.

Accommodation   Fédération Nationale des Logis et Auberges de France,
     25 rue Jean-Mermoz, 75008 Paris; 359—86—67.
Fédération Nationale des Gîtes Ruraux,
     35 rue G-de-Mauroy, 75009 Paris.
Fédération Unie des Auberges de Jeunesse,
     6 rue Mesnil, 75106 Paris.
Youth Hostels Association, 14 Southampton Street,
     London WC2E 7HY.
Amis des Routiers, 354 Fulham Road,
     London SW10 9UH.
Castels et Camping Caravanning,
     169 avenue Victor-Hugo, 75116 Paris.
Fédération Nationale de l'Hôtellerie de Plein Air
     (FNHPA) 10 rue de l'Isly, 75008 Paris

Touring Club de France, 65 avenue de la Grande Armée,   **Driving**
   75106 Paris; 532—22—15.
Centre National d'Information Routière, 858—33—33.
Centre des Renseignements des Autoroutes, 705—90—01.

Fédération Française de Cycloto-Tourisme,   **Other means**
   8 rue Jean Marie Jego, 75013 Paris.   **of transport**
Cyclists' Touring Club, 69 Meadrow, Godalming, Surrey.
Comité Nationale des Sentiers de Grande Randonnée,
   92 rue de Clignancourt, 75883 Paris.
Syndicat National des Loueurs de Bateaux de Plaisance,
   port de la Bourdonnais, 75007 Paris.
Editions Maritimes et d'Outre-Mer,
   77 rue Jacob, 75006 Paris.
Royal Yachting Association, Victoria Way, Woking,
   Surrey GU21 1EQ.
Provoya, 65 passage Brady, 75010 Paris; 246—00—66.

Union Nationale des Centres Sportifs de Plein Air   **Sport**
   (UNCSPA), 62 rue de la Glacière, 75013 Paris.
Club Alpin Francais, 7 rue de la Boétie, 75008 Paris.
Fédération Française d'Etudes et de Sports Sous-Marins,
   34 rue du Colisée, 75008 Paris.
Association Nationale pour le Tourisme Equestre,
   12 rue du Parc Royal, 75003 Paris.

French and International Road Signs

accotements non stabilisés	soft verges (or non-existent edges)
allumez vos phares	switch on headlights
autres directions	through traffic
bifurcation	junction, fork
boue	mud on roads
carrefour	crossroads
cédez le passage	give way, yield
centre ville	town centre
chaussée déformée/ défoncée	bad road surface (no mention of temporary)
chaussée glissante rétrécie	slippery surface/road narrows
chute de pierres	falling stones (a hazard after they have fallen on the road rather than when they are falling from above)

círcuit touristique	scenic route
démunie de bandes axiales	no road markings
déviation	diversion
feux (de circulation)	traffic lights
file de droite/gauche	right/left-hand lane
fin de chantier	road clear
giratoire	roundabout
gravillons	loose chippings
impasse	dead end
interdit de doubler	no overtaking
itinéraire bis	alternative route
marquage horizontal effacé	no road markings
nids de poule	potholes (literally chicken nests)
passage à niveau/piétons	level/pedestrian crossing
passage protégé	your right of way
péage	toll
poids lourds	(route for) heavy goods vehicles
priorité à droite	priority to the right
ralentir	slow down
rappel	remember (speed limit)
réservé aux autobus/ cyclistes	bus/cycle lane
risque d'inondation	road liable to flooding
rives dangereuses	dangerous verges
rond point	roundabout
route barrée/inondée	road closed/flooded
sauf riverains	access/residents only
sens interdit/unique	no entry/one way
serrez à droite	keep right
sortie de camions/d'usine	lorry (truck)/factory exit
STOP	stop
toutes directions	through traffic
travaux	road works
troupeaux	cattle crossing
véhicules lents	slow vehicles
verglas	icy surface
virages	bends
vitesse limitée	speed limit
voie sans issue	no through road
zone commerciale/ industrielle/ piétonnière	commercial zone (for hyper-market)/industrial zone/ pedestrian precinct

Conversion Tables

Distance 1 kilometre = 0.62 miles
1 mile = 1.61 km
    Roughly:
    1 km   5/8 mile
    3 km   2 miles
    5 km   3 miles
    8 km   5 miles
    10 km 6 miles

Weight 100 grammes = 3.33 oz; 1 kilogramme (1000 g) = 2.2 lb
1 oz = 28.35 g; 1 lb = 0.45 kg
    Roughly:
    100 g   just under ¼ lb
    250 g   ½ lb
    500 g   1 lb
    1 kg   just over 2 lb

Liquid 1 litre (100 centilitres/1000 cubic centimetres) = 1.76
    imperial pints/2.11 US pints
1 imp. pint = 0.57 litres; 1 imp. gallon = 4.55 litres
1 US pint = 0.47 litres; 1 US gallon = 3.79 litres
    Roughly:
    0.5 litres   just under 1 imp. pint/just over 1 US pint
    1 litre   just under 2 imp. pints/just over 2 US pints
    3.75 litres 1 US gallon
    4.5 litres   1 imp. gallon

Length 1 centimetre = 0.39 inches; 1 metre (100 centimetres)
    = 39.37 inches/1.094 yards
    Roughly:
    5 cm   2 inches
    1 metre just over 1 yard

centigrade °	fahrenheit °		Temperature
100	212 boiling point		
38	100		
30	86		
25	77		
20	68		
15	59		
10	50		
5	41		
0	32 freezing point		

For a quick rough conversion from C° to F°, double the centigrade figure and add 30.

Women's dresses	UK	USA	France	Clothing
	10	8	36	
	12	10	38	
	14	12	40	
	16	14	42	
	18	16	44	
	20	18	46	

Men's shirts	UK/USA		France
	14		36
	14½		37
	15		38
	15½		39
	16		41
	16½		42
	17		43
	17½		44

Shoes	UK	USA	France
	3	4½	35/36
	4	5½	37
	5	6½	38
	6	7½	39
	7	8½	40/41
	8	9½	41/42
	9	10½	42/43
	10	11½	43/44
	11	12½	44/45
	12	14	45/46

NORD
Pas-de-Calais
Nord
Somme Aisne
PICARDIE
Seine-Maritime
Oise Ardennes Moselle
HAUTE-NORMANDIE **LORRAINE**
Manche Calvados Région Meuse Meurthe-et-Moselle
Eure Parisienne Marne Moselle Bas-Rhin
BASSE-NORMANDIE **ÎLE DE FRANCE** **CHAMPAGNE** **ALSACE**
Orne Eure-et-Loir Seine-et-Marne Aube Haut-Rhin
Eure-et-Loir Vosges
Finistère Côtes-du-Nord Ille-et-Vilaine Mayenne Sarthe Loiret Yonne Haute-Marne Tre-de-Belfort
BRETAGNE **PAYS DE LA LOIRE** **CENTRE** **BOURGOGNE** **FRANCHE-COMTÉ**
Morbihan Haute-Saône
Loire-Atlantique Indre-et-Loire Loir-et-Cher Cher Nièvre Côte-d'Or Doubs
Maine-et-Loire Indre Allier Saône-et-Loire Jura
Vendée Deux-Sèvres Vienne Creuse Ain Haute-Savoie
POITOU-CHARENTES **LIMOUSIN** Puy-de-Dôme Rhône Savoie
Charente-Maritime Haute-Vienne **AUVERGNE** Loire **RHÔNE-ALPES**
Charente Corrèze Cantal Haute-Loire Ardèche Isère
Gironde Dordogne Lot Lozère Drôme Hautes-Alpes
AQUITAINE Lot-et-Garonne **MIDI-PYRÉNÉES** Aveyron Gard Vaucluse Alpes-de-Hte-Provence Alpes-Maritimes
Landes Tarn-et-Garonne Tarn **LANGUEDOC** Bouches-du-Rhône Var **PROVENCE-CÔTE D'AZUR**
Gers Haute-Garonne Hérault
Pyrénées-Atlantiques Aude
Hautes-Pyrénées Ariège Pyrénées-Orientales
Haute-Corse
CORSE
Corse du Sud

━ ━ ━ Regional boundaries
-------- Département boundaries

Regions of France

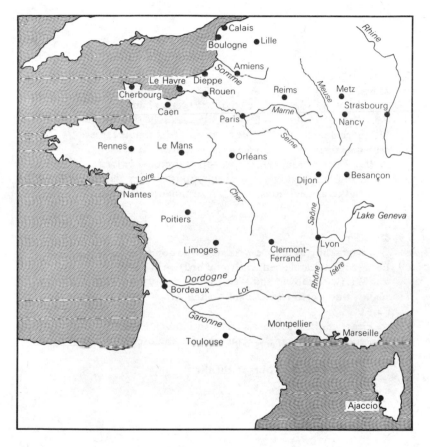

Major towns of France

Sample Hotel
Reservation Letter

Monsieur

Je voudrais réserver une chambre (deux chambres) à deux lits (avec un grand lit, à un lit) avec salle de bains et WC (avec douche et WC) pour une nuit (deux nuits, une semaine, deux semaines) le *date* (à partir du *date*).

Veuillez confirmer la réservation et indiquer le tarif des chambres. Ci-joint un coupon-réponse international.

Veuillez agréer, Monsieur, mes sentiments distingués.

Dear Sir

I would like to reserve a room (two rooms) with twin beds (with a double bed, with one bed) with bathroom and WC (with shower and WC) for one night (two nights, one week, two weeks) on the *date* (from the *date*).

Please confirm the reservation and indicate the terms. An international reply coupon is enclosed.

Yours faithfully

Index

Suggestions

This page can be used to send in your suggestions for improving the book. What vital matters have been overlooked? What difficulties and pitfalls have been neglected or glossed over? What else should the intending visitor know about the quirks of the French way of life? Please write and tell us.

If your suggestions are adopted in a revised edition, you will receive a free copy in recognition of your services in helping other people cope with France.

Please send your suggestions to Fay Sharman, c/o Basil Blackwell Ltd, 108 Cowley Road, Oxford OX4 1JF.

Name . . . .

Address . . . .

. . . .

My suggestions are